ENJOY

Gourmet Every Day

Shawna -

Happy Cooking !

Best -

Catherine & Jane !

ENJOY

Gourmet Every Day

CATHERINE BERGEN

WITH
JULIA SCANNELL

GOURMET | FEATURING
TULOCAY'S
MADE IN
NAPA VALLEY | PANTRY

JANE!

MADE IN *Napa Valley* JANE!®

Made In Napa Valley
A Division of Tulocay & Company, Inc.
Napa, California
www.madeinnapavalley.com
888.627.2859
FIRST EDITION

Art Direction: Julia Scannell
Photography: Dan Mills
Food Stylist: Kim Konecny/Food Stylist Assistant: Julia Skahill
Copyeditor: Julie Stillman
Production Artist: Paul Bailey
Additional photographs by Kathryn Martin (pages vi, viii, 6, 8,
12, 14, 22, 32, 33, 42, 62, 72, 98, 112, 116, 132, 140, 141, 150 & 160)
and Nanci Kerby (page 130)

Printed In Hong Kong by Global Interprint, Inc, Santa Rosa, California

ISBN 0-9788490-0-0
Library of Congress Control Number: 20066931739

10 9 8 7 6 5 4 5 2 1

*This book is dedicated to everyone on the Tulocay team and to all those
who have been on the team over the years including my brother, Chris. And to Dick and Howard
who understood and now share my vision. Thank you for helping me realize my dream
because without all of you, none of this would have come to be!
I am forever grateful.*

JANE!®

Acknowledgments

I have been fortunate to have hired some fabulous people over the years. Carlos Segura and Rafael Hernandez were two of the first people to join the team and have jumped in and helped the company as it has grown and changed. Today Carlos is in charge of all production including the warehouse and shipping, and Rapha is in charge of the actual cooking and getting all the products into the jars and bottles. They basically run the back of the house with their team of manufacturing professionals, including Marina Lopez, Manuel Segura, Maria Arreola, Rosa Torres, and all of my amigos that have been with us for years and for whom I am extremely grateful.

When we had reached a point where we needed a greater level of expertise in product development and how we did purchasing and inventory, Michael Garza and Jim Lipman, both from Cal Poly, joined the team. Michael is our product developer and creator of all the fabulous formulations of products for both our line and our private-label customers and Jim handles operations and IT. They continue to do an amazing job!

At the same time that we were creating our product line, Leslie Krzan joined us and started helping with customer service and general office work. Although she would be just perfect on the customer service team (and believe me I tried to sway her there), her passion is numbers, and with Keyri Candray's help, she runs the financial and administrative part of the business. And they do an excellent job!

As the line started to grow, we wanted to help people everywhere understand all the terrific and easy things you could make with our products. I met Julia Scannell, a local artist with a great passion for food and a whole lot of creative talent, and she started working with us as a freelancer, creating and photographing recipes for our website. After about a year, I begged her to come on board. Not wanting to give up her freedom, I convinced her that this would be a good thing and she is now our Creative Director. She is responsible for our entire look and feel, and as you can see from this book, again I am extremely lucky.

Our team is continuing to grow with extremely talented people and we are so lucky now to have Tammy Scorza, Lela Adelman, and Karen Foley join us. Their talents will help us bring more *Made In Napa Valley* to your table with new products and recipes. In the fall of 2007, we are opening the Made In Napa Valley C.A.F.E. (Culinary Artisan Food Experience). You will be able to enjoy our food, see our manufacturing process, and participate in classes that will teach you more about food, wine, and easy entertaining in the Napa Valley lifestyle while having a whole lot of fun! We hope you will come and visit.

JANE!®

Contents

Introduction

As far back as I can remember I have always loved food. I started learning to cook when I was five. Pancakes were my first experience at the stove—I was fascinated by the fact that when the batter bubbled it was my cue to turn them over. Of course I loved to eat them too! When I was twelve, my mother gave me $25 to go shopping at the mall for school clothes. The first thing I did was go order a grilled cheese sandwich and an Orange Julius and then went to the bookstore and bought three cookbooks. Needless to say, my mother was not pleased, but I read those books cover to cover many times. It has always been about food for me.

I have done all kinds of things in my life: groomed dogs, gone to cosmetology school, sold life and health insurance, and was a licensed stock broker and real estate agent. I also did accounting for a restaurant, worked as an assistant manager in a clothing store, waited tables, tended bar, sold graphics and printing, and I am sure there were other things that I can't even remember! But nothing made my heart sing. When I was 37 years old, I went to a lecture in Los Angeles, and Maryanne Williamson said, "Do what you love and the money will come." Although I had no formal culinary training, I knew that I wanted to do something with food and wine. I was ready for a change and I wondered where the right place to go was. And since food and wine go together, I thought Napa Valley, and after a short, three-day visit, with about $800 in my pocket and a burning desire to succeed, I rented a U-haul truck and moved to the Napa Valley.

A BRIEF HISTORY OF
TULOCAY & COMPANY, INC.

With a little luck and a whole lot of passion to create a specialty food company, Tulocay Foods was born just three months later. A lot of people asked why I chose the name Tulocay. I didn't want the name of my company to be "Catherine's Oils and Vinegars," how boring. And one day during the development phase, I was driving across the Imola Bridge in Napa and saw a sign that said Tulocay Creek. I thought "Tulocay, that's a pretty word." I did a little research and found out it was a Pomo Indian word that meant red. And then I discovered that in the Napa Valley, there is a Tulocay Winery, (owned by a great guy, Bill Cadman), a Tulocay Cemetary, and back in the 1800s there was a Spanish land grant called Rancho Tulocay. So after about a year, in 1995 we incorporated and became Tulocay & Company, Inc.

We started out with private label oil and vinegar products for the wineries and in a very short amount of time, we landed some large national accounts that really helped put us on the map.

After about six years of doing oil and vinegar every way one could imagine and private label only, I really wanted to start making sauces and condiments and offer a line of food that truly reflected who we were. Tulocay & Company had three goals in developing our food line.

First we wanted to create a product line that was all about quality—great flavor combinations inspired by the abundance and beauty of the Napa Valley. We wanted a way to share this wonderful region and its world-class wines, fabulous restaurants, and bounty of fresh produce. Not everyone is as lucky as we are to live here, but we wanted to make products that would allow people everywhere to have a little Napa Valley on their table no matter where they lived.

Next, we wanted all-natural, shelf-stable products that tasted and looked homemade. We came up with: savory sauces and tapenades that are thick and chunky; rubs, marinades, grilling glazes, mustards, fruit balsamics and dipping oils that are jam-packed with flavor; and decadent dessert sauces that are so good they sometimes get eaten right out of the jar!

Our final goal was to make food that would allow people to enjoy gourmet every day, hence our tag-line and the title of our book. We wanted to make products that do most of the work for you. How great would it be if all you had to do is open a jar or a spice tin, pair it with a carbohydrate or a protein and maybe a few other ingredients, and you have a great tasting gourmet dish with very little effort?

In just one year, after a whole lot of testing, tasting, and experimenting, *Tulocay's Made in Napa Valley* came to fruition in July of 2001. We launched our product line at the New York Fancy Food Show with 40 products (I must have been out of my mind but I just didn't know any better) and we were nominated for the National Association of the Specialty Food Trade's (NASFT) Outstanding Product Line award that year. We didn't win, but the fact that we were nominated for the most prestigious award in the industry and hadn't sold a jar yet was pretty darned exciting. After being nominated, I got a taste of winning and I wanted that award for myself and my team because to me it meant being recognized by my peers as one of the best. I am delighted to say that we did take the gold and are the proud recipients of the NASFT's Outstanding Product Line 2004 award!

ABOUT THIS BOOK

I get a lot of requests for a cookbook and finally decided to write it so that my team and I could share our vision for the food we make. This book and our products are all about helping you make delicious, healthy meals every day in a very short amount of time and we give you unique and fun recipes to entertain with confidence and ease. Whether it is Monday night after a long day at work, a Saturday-night sit-down dinner party, or casually hanging out with family and friends (as we do a lot here in the Napa Valley), these are dishes you will be proud to serve. Not only do they look spectacular and taste outrageously good, but they are also on the healthy side—and you are the only who needs to know how easily they all came together.

TIPS FOR BECOMING AN EVERY DAY GOURMET

Here are some pointers for getting the most out of the recipes in the book.

 The great thing about this book is that you can be part of our culinary team. Nothing is set in stone. Feel free to experiment! If you don't eat beef, in most cases you can substitute chicken, pork, fish, or tofu. If you don't like Brussels sprouts, use green beans or asparagus.

Feel free to swap out products. For instance, for the Asian Potato Salad, if you don't have the *Asian Accents Herb Rub*, use the *Napa Valley Meritage Herb Rub* or *Mediterranean Herb Rub* or any of the rubs for that matter; you will have a whole new recipe. Or if you don't have our dipping oil or mustard for instance, use one that you do have.

You may notice that a lot of the recipes are cooked on high heat. That is because I don't like overcooked or dried-out foods. It is also a lot quicker and helps keep in the flavors.

In the Napa Valley, we like to grill and dine al fresco almost all year, but if you don't live in one of those places, a grill pan that you can use on the stovetop is a great alternative to an outdoor grill. They are super for panini, too.

My bread of choice is tortillas. I eat them for breakfast, lunch, and dinner. So I recommend that you keep some on hand for a quick delicious meal and a great way to create fun leftovers and interesting wraps.

I am one of those people who like to go to the grocery store every day just because I like grocery stores (surprise surprise). I check them out when I travel even when I can't cook anything. However, I have found that there are some items that you should keep on hand so you can create easy, healthy, quick meals anytime or whip up a quick appetizer when people just pop in.

Of course I recommend lots of *Made in Napa Valley* products in your kitchen, along with items like canned tuna (I like the Italian stuff), canned salmon, dried pastas and rice, canned beans (like lentils, black and white beans) and some kind of stock (chicken, beef, or vegetable). Also some good olive oil, a couple of cheeses, some nuts, and frozen puff pastry is a must! Oh, and a couple bottles of wine.

WINE SUGGESTIONS

We also include wine suggestions in the book that were graciously written by the "COPIA WineGuys" Peter Marks and Burke Owens, at COPIA, the American Center for Wine, Food & the Arts located in Napa. COPIA, the vision and the dream of Robert and Margrit Mondavi, offers fun and interactive programs, tastings, exhibitions, festivals, dining, performances, and organic gardens. Peter and Burke are extremely good at what they do and together, they have over 50 years experience in the wine business. They offer wine-pairing ideas for each of our products and many of the recipes accompanying them. We believe the best wine and the right wine to go with your meal is the wine you like!

NUTRITIONAL INFORMATION

We believe in using the freshest ingredients both in our products and in our recipes. Healthy cooking and eating is what we strive for and we follow the "everything in moderation" strategy. If counting calories or carbs is important to you, you can find the nutritional analysis for each recipe on our website **madeinnapa-valley.com**.

When cooking and entertaining, be sure to have fun, be yourself, and don't be afraid to try new things. If you want to share your experiences and creations with us or have comments or suggestions, we would be thrilled to hear from you! Feel free to shoot me an email and I will get back to you. Who knows, we may put your recipe in our next book (with your permission of course). I am excited about sharing my passion for food and the Napa Valley with you. Happy cooking and be sure to enjoy Gourmet Every Day!

Jane!

When I started to put together my specialty food line, I didn't have a name or a logo. At the same time I got a Jack Russell terrier, who my friend Mark named Jane. Jane Russell, get it?

From the beginning Jane has come to the office every day with me and is very popular. She has a personality that just won't quit and is thrilled when people come to visit. It's amazing how many people bring her treats.

As the product line was developing, we had picked out the packaging and the name but I couldn't come up with a logo that I was excited about or that really reflected who we were. One day I thought hey, let's put Jane on the label. We did and it looked great. Someone walked in to the office and Jane got so excited I thought, we have to add an exclamation point. So her name became Jane!. At first people said "Oh that's cute but you really aren't going to put your dog on the label of a human food line are you?" I thought why not, I couldn't think of anything that I liked better, so it stuck!

Personally Jane! is a big part of my life. She is my running partner (I can always count on her to show up when I do) and we run 4 to 6 miles, up and down the hills surrounded by vineyards.

We have so much fun including her in the photo shoots. I swear she knows when she is being photographed. She has become quite the supermodel and definitely works for food. Jane! keeps us all entertained for sure and is definably a big part of the Tulocay Team!

UNITY IS STRENGTH...
WHEN THERE IS
TEAMWORK AND COLLABORATION,
WONDERFUL THINGS CAN
BE ACHIEVED.

Mattie Stepanek

Cookbook Team

JULIA SCANNELL ART DIRECTOR

Food and design are creative passions of Julia Scannell's and after over 20 years working as a graphic designer she has found a position that allows her to fulfill both as Creative Director for Tulocay & Co, Inc. She began her career as a book designer and moved into corporate design for hi-tech and financial companies such as Oracle and Visa. In 1998, she moved from San Francisco to Napa which brought with it creative opportunities with the wine industry and the chance to reconnect with her fine art interest. She has developed recipes for two cookbooks prior to meeting Catherine Bergen and creating recipes using *Made In Napa Valley* pantry products. Like Catherine's Jack Russell terrier Jane!, Julia's dog Otto — a 2-year-old rescue — loves photo shoots, even if he is cropped out of a shot.

DAN MILLS PHOTOGRAPHER

Dan Mills is an advertising and corporate photographer specializing in the wine and food industry. For the past twenty five years he has worked for clients including Apple Computer, CitiCorp, Diageo, Fosters, Kendall-Jackson, Chronicle Books, Sutter Home, Time Magazine, Foster Farms, and the Food Network. His Napa Valley studio features a kitchen set, a full prep kitchen, an organic culinary garden, and a small winery. Molly, his five-year-old English Lab accompanies him to the studio and loves all food types, occasionally hunts pheasants, and loves to body surf in the ocean.

KIM KONECNY FOOD STYLIST
JULIA SKAHILL FOOD STYLIST ASSISTANT

Deciding to change careers in her late twenties Kim Konecny followed her lifelong passion for food and graduated from Tante Marie's Cooking School in San Francisco in 1995. She pursued food-styling positions in order to learn the trade and discovered her true calling in life. Kim has had the opportunity to work with a diverse clientele, from design and publishing firms to electronic media and the film industry. She has been the food stylist on more than 50 cookbooks.

Originally from New Zealand, Julia Skahill moved to New York City in 1998 and along with two partners, began a corporate catering and event-planning company, which she ran for seven years. After selling her business to move to San Francisco, a fateful connection led her to Kim Konecny. She knew she made the right decision and Julia has been assisting Kim since April 2006.

PETER MARKS & BURKE OWENS "COPIA WINEGUYS"

Director of Wine Peter Marks holds the prestigious "Master of Wine" (MW) title and "Madame Bollenger Foundation Award," bestowed to the Master of Wine with the highest tasting score. Associate Director of Wine Burke Owens was nominated for a James Beard Foundation Award for Outstanding Wine Service and won *San Francisco Chronicle's* "Best Bay Area Wine Service" three years running for his work as a sommelier extraordinaire. Together, they have over 50 years experience in the wine business. They offer insights into wine selection and priceless tips on food and wine pairing.

Sunrise over the
vineyards along the
Silverado Trail in Napa
provides a gorgeous setting
for Jane! and me to go for
an early morning run

Menu

ASIAN PICNIC

Caramelized Asian Chicken Wings   145

Asian Potato Salad   87

Shrimp and Vegetable Summer Rolls   57

Asian Broccoli Slaw 56

Sandwich Cookies with Chocolate & Pecans   149

✻

NAPA VALLEY BREAKFAST

Breakfast Turkey Sausage   77

Scrambled Eggs with Herbs & Goat Cheese   94

Grilled Bread with Tomatoes & Shaved Manchego   28

✻

A PACFIC RIM DINNER PARTY

Sesame Swordfish Skewers with Dipping Sauce   59

Chicken Coconut Milk Soup   87

Watercress, Cabbage Salad with Apples & Walnuts   20

Ginger-Soy Hanger Steak   55

Asian Noodles   57

Pear Tarts with Carmel Sauce   144

✻

DINNER IN BAJA ON THE BEACH

Roasted Corn and Red Bell Pepper Scoops   123

Chile & Citrus Crab Cocktails   61

Fiesta Guacamole   90

Fabulous Fish Tacos   91

Southwest Stuffed Chile Peppers   109

Black Bean and Charred Corn Salad with Avocado   90

Banana-Pecan Crepes with Caramel Sauce   145

Grapes

THE BEGINNING OF A
NEW VINTAGE
AT STONY HILL VINEYARDS
IN ST. HELENA

CHAPTER 1

Vinaigrettes

LEMON DILL VINAIGRETTE WITH CHARDONNAY

Green Beans with Slivered Almonds

Braised Halibut with Leeks & Mushrooms

Chicken Brochettes with Lemon & Cherry Tomatoes

Lemon Dill Artichokes

MERLOT VINAIGRETTE WITH WALNUT OIL

Roasted Olives

Watercress-Cabbage Salad with Apples & Walnuts

Heirloom Tomato Salad with Mozzarella

Mixed Greens with Cranberries, Blue Cheese & Pecans

LEMON DILL VINAIGRETTE WITH CHARDONNAY

THERE'S NOTHING BETTER THAN A SALAD MADE WITH REALLY GOOD DRESSING, AND THIS ONE MAKES IT EASY. DON'T LIMIT YOUR USE TO SALADS; TRY IT AS A MARINADE FOR CHICKEN, WHITE FISH, OR SHRIMP — DELICIOUS!

GREEN BEANS WITH SLIVERED ALMONDS

1 tablespoon olive oil

1 shallot, diced

1 pound green beans
(or combination of green, purple, and wax beans), stem tips removed

2 tablespoons slivered almonds

⅓ cup *Lemon Dill Vinaigrette with Chardonnay*

Salt (preferably kosher or sea salt) and freshly ground pepper

Heat the oil in a large sauté pan over medium-high heat. Add beans and sauté for 3 minutes, stirring frequently. Add the shallots and sauté until they are golden, about 2 minutes, stirring frequently. Add the almonds and cook 1 minute more (beans should have golden brown spots in some areas and still be crisp but cooked through); remove from heat.

Carefully stir the *Lemon Dill Vinaigrette with Chardonnay* into the bean mixture (the hot pan may cause it to spatter) and add salt and pepper to taste. Serve warm.

Serves 4 as a side dish

18

BRAISED HALIBUT WITH LEEKS & MUSHROOMS

Light and flavorful, this dish makes me feel like spring is in the air any time of year!

6 tablespoons *Lemon Dill Vinaigrette with Chardonnay*

1 large leek, white part only, rinsed well, halved lengthwise, and cut into ¼-inch slices

½ pound any combination of wild mushrooms, sliced

Salt (preferably kosher or sea salt) and freshly ground pepper

¼ cup water

½ cup white wine or vegetable broth

4 halibut fillets (about 2 pounds), bones and skin removed

12 asparagus spears cut on the diagonal in 1-inch pieces

In a large skillet over medium heat, combine 2 tablespoons of the *Lemon Dill Vinaigrette with Chardonnay* with the leeks, cover, and cook 3 minutes. Do not let leeks brown. Add the mushrooms, a little salt and pepper, and the water; cover and cook for 3 minutes. Add the wine and let simmer for 3 minutes uncovered.

Season both sides of the fish with salt and pepper and place on top of the vegetables in the pan. Pour 1 tablespoon of the *Vinaigrette* over each fillet, cover, and cook for 5 minutes. Place the asparagus around the fish, cover, and cook for 5 minutes. The fish is cooked through when it is opaque in the center. Serve the halibut with the vegetables and juices spooned on top.

Serves 4

CHICKEN BROCHETTES WITH LEMON & CHERRY TOMATOES

Brochettes are fun to do for a crowd because you can make them up ahead of time or have the ingredients prepped and let the kids put them together. They love to help! These may be grilled or broiled.

1½ pounds boneless, skinless chicken breasts cut into 1-inch cubes

16 cherry tomatoes

½ red onion, cut into 1-inch pieces

1 lemon, cut into slices and halved

16 basil leaves

Salt (preferably kosher or sea salt) and freshly ground pepper

½ cup *Lemon Dill Vinaigrette with Chardonnay*

8 wooden skewers, soaked in water for 30 minutes

Prepare the grill. In a large bowl, combine the chicken cubes, tomatoes, onions, a couple of pinches of salt and pepper, and the *Lemon Dill Vinaigrette with Chardonnay* and stir to coat well. Thread each skewer with alternating chicken, tomatoes, onions, basil leaves, and lemon slices. You are looking for variety in color and ingredients when threading the skewers. Grill for 4-6 minutes per side or until chicken is cooked through. Serve piled onto a bright-colored platter with couscous to soak up the juices.

Note: For broiling: place the skewers on a foil-lined baking sheet and follow the directions for grilling.

Serves 4

LEMON DILL ARTICHOKES

My Mom cooked artichokes with a little lemon and served them with mayonnaise. I tried them with this dressing and I think my Mom would have agreed that this is fabulous!

½ cup mayonnaise

1 clove garlic, minced

Salt (preferably kosher or sea salt)

1¼ cups *Lemon Dill Vinaigrette with Chardonnay*

2 large artichokes

In a small bowl, mix together the mayonnaise, garlic, and a pinch of salt. Refrigerate for at least an hour before serving.

Use a sharp knife to trim the artichoke stalks close to the base so they sit upright. Cut the top ¾ inch off the tops. Gently push open the artichoke leaves and pour ½ cup of the *Lemon Dill Vinaigrette with Chardonnay* into the center of each artichoke.

Fill a pot large enough to hold the artichokes upright with 1½ inches of water. Salt the water, bring to a boil, add the artichokes, cover, and reduce heat to low. Cook for approximately 40 minutes depending on the size of the artichokes. They are done when you can easily pull a leaf from the center of the artichoke. To serve, place the artichokes on a platter and spoon 2 tablespoons of *Vinaigrette* over the top of each one, sprinkle with a little salt, and serve with garlic mayonnaise.

Serves 4-6 as an appetizer

Wine Suggestions

Bright and zesty, this vinaigrette is exactly what you need when pouring a Sauvignon Blanc—crisp acidity layered with fresh herbs! Pinot Grigio will hold its own but a Sauvignon Blanc from Napa, Sancerre or New Zealand will make a marvelous match.

An Albariño from Spain is especially good with the halibut and asparagus. Try a rich, but not oaky, California Chardonnay with the artichoke dish. The use of mayonnaise as a dip will soften this cruciferous vegetable's hard edge.

MERLOT VINAIGRETTE WITH WALNUT OIL

It can be difficult to find a good bottled salad dressing, but we think this is an exception. The red wine, walnut oil, and herbs are a delicious combination, perfect for salad greens. We also like to get creative and use this *Vinaigrette* in recipes other than salads.

ROASTED OLIVES

1 pound mixed olives
(kalamata, niçoise, picholine, etc.)

¼ cup *Merlot Vinaigrette with Walnut Oil*

2 teaspoons fennel seeds

Zest from 1 orange

1 bay leaf

Preheat the oven to 350°F. In a small baking dish, combine all the ingredients and stir to mix well. Bake until the olives are hot, about 15 minutes. Serve with focaccia, spiced nuts, cheeses, dried fruits, and cured meats for an impromptu snack or meal. (The olives will keep in a covered container in the refrigerator; reheat before serving.)

Serves 4-6 as part of an appetizer platter

WATERCRESS-CABBAGE SALAD WITH APPLES & WALNUTS

Autumn flavors like apples and walnuts make this a nice alternative to serve with roast chicken or turkey. I enjoy salads like this one served on chilled plates with chilled forks, so about an hour before serving place the salad plates and forks in the freezer. It's the little things!

4 cups shredded Napa cabbage (about half of a medium-sized head)

¼ pound watercress or arugula

1 crunchy red apple cut into thin julienne strips

¼ pound soft fresh goat cheese, crumbled

½ cup walnut halves, toasted (optional)

4-6 tablespoons *Merlot Vinaigrette with Walnut Oil*

Freshly ground pepper

In a large bowl, combine the cabbage, watercress, apple, goat cheese, and walnuts. Pour the desired amount of *Merlot Vinaigrette with Walnut Oil* (I like my salads lightly dressed) over the salad ingredients and toss gently to mix well. Divide the salad among four salad plates and top with a couple of grinds of fresh black pepper.

Serves 4

HEIRLOOM TOMATO SALAD WITH MOZZARELLA

This salad definitely reminds me of summer, when vine-ripened tomatoes are abundant and the mozzarella is fresh. Serve family style alongside a big platter of grilled chicken on a warm night!

> 4 tomatoes, sliced
>
> 1 pound buffalo mozzarella, sliced
>
> Bunch of fresh basil leaves or arugula
>
> *Merlot Vinaigrette with Walnut Oil*
>
> Salt (preferably kosher or sea salt)

Arrange the tomatoes, mozzarella, and basil on individual plates or on a large platter, alternating and overlapping them. Drizzle with the *Merlot Vinaigrette with Walnut Oil* (shake well before drizzling) and a pinch of salt. Serve immediately.

Serves 4-6

Tip: Always serve tomatoes at room temperature for maximum flavor.

MIXED GREENS WITH CRANBERRIES, BLUE CHEESE & PECANS

For potlucks and get-togethers, I am always asked to bring the salad. This is one of my favorites! Feel free to substitute tomatoes, pears, or whatever is in season for the cranberries, or just omit the fruit altogether.

> 2 cups mixed field greens
>
> 2 cups chopped hearts of romaine lettuce
>
> $\frac{1}{3}$ cup chopped green onions (white and green parts)
>
> $\frac{1}{3}$ cup crumbled blue cheese
>
> $\frac{1}{3}$ cup dried cranberries
>
> $\frac{1}{3}$ cup pecan halves, toasted
>
> 4–6 tablespoons *Merlot Vinaigrette with Walnut Oil*

In a large bowl combine the field greens, romaine, onions, blue cheese, cranberries and pecans. Pour the desired amount of *Merlot Vinaigrette with Walnut Oil* (I like my salads lightly dressed) over the salad ingredients and toss to mix well. Divide the salad among four chilled salad plates.

Serves 4

Olives

An ancient grove of
olive trees prospering on the
Turley Wine Cellars property

CHAPTER 2

Dipping Oils

CLASSIC DIPPING OIL WITH BALSAMIC

Roasted Beets

Italian Tuna & White Bean Salad

Four-Cheese Pizza

Prosciutto-Wrapped Asparagus with Melon

✤

GARDEN HERB DIPPING OIL WITH BALSAMIC

Grilled Bread with Tomatoes & Shaved Manchego

My Favorite Bread Salad

Watermelon-Tomato Surprise

Pasta Primavera

✤

GARLIC PARMESAN DIPPING OIL WITH CAPERS

Bruschetta with Garden Tomatoes & Shaved Parmesan

Garlic Shrimp Fettuccine

Summer Pasta with Grilled Chicken & Vegetables

Brussels Sprouts with Prosciutto

JANE!®

CLASSIC DIPPING OIL WITH BALSAMIC

We combine extra-virgin olive oil and balsamic vinegar to create this classic dipping oil. It offers such versatility — use it for dipping crusty bread, for stir-frying and roasting vegetables, or stirring into pasta with some grated Parmesan cheese.

ROASTED BEETS

2 pounds medium-sized beets

¼ cup olive oil

1 teaspoon salt (preferably kosher or sea salt)

½-¾ cup *Classic Dipping Oil with Balsamic*

Preheat the oven to 400°F. Rinse and dry the beets, leaving the skin on. In a large bowl, toss the beets with the olive oil and salt. Arrange on a greased baking sheet. Roast for 20-40 minutes, depending on the size of the beets; the largest beet should be tender to the center when pierced with the tip of a knife. Remove from the oven and cool.

Using a small, sharp knife, remove the skins, and cut beets into ⅜-inch-thick slices. Transfer the beets to a bowl and toss gently with the *Classic Dipping Oil with Balsamic*. Serve at room temperature or chilled. Add some crumbled feta or soft fresh goat cheese for a delicious flavor combination.

Serves 4-6

ITALIAN TUNA & WHITE BEAN SALAD

This is so delicious you won't believe it is actually healthy! You may want to keep your pantry stocked with cans of white beans and tuna along with the Classic Dipping Oil with Balsamic *for creating a fabulous salad for impromptu lunch guests.*

> One 15-ounce can white beans (cannellini or navy beans)
>
> 6 ounces canned Italian tuna packed in oil, drained (or domestic tuna)
>
> ⅓ cup diced sun-dried tomatoes
>
> ¼ cup minced fresh basil leaves
>
> ⅓ cup *Classic Dipping Oil with Balsamic*
>
> Salt (preferably kosher or sea salt) and freshly ground pepper
>
> 4 large butter lettuce leaves
>
> ¼ cup shaved Parmesan cheese

Combine the beans, tuna, sun-dried tomatoes, basil, *Classic Dipping Oil with Balsamic*, and salt and pepper to taste. To serve, spoon one-quarter of the salad into each of the lettuce leaves and top with the Parmesan.

Variation: You can turn this salad into bruschetta appetizers by spooning it onto toasted slices of sourdough bread, topping with Parmesan, and broiling for a minute or two until the cheese melts.

Serves 4 as a side dish or appetizer

FOUR-CHEESE PIZZA

This is for the cheese lovers for sure. Serve as an appetizer for three or four people or add a tossed green salad and a glass of wine and you have a fabulous dinner for two!

> One 16-ounce prebaked thin pizza crust
> ¼ cup shredded Fontina cheese
> ¼ cup shredded Asiago cheese
> ¼ cup shredded mozzarella cheese
> ¼ cup shredded Parmesan cheese
> *Classic Dipping Oil with Balsamic,* for drizzling

Preheat the oven to 450°F. Sprinkle the cheeses on the pizza crust (add more cheese if you like it really cheesy). Bake until cheese is bubbly and starting to turn golden brown in spots and the crust is crispy, about 12-15 minutes. Remove the pizza from oven, drizzle with a couple tablespoons of *Classic Dipping Oil with Balsamic,* cut into wedges, and serve.

Makes one 12-inch pizza

Wine Suggestions

Never fear pairing wine with vinegar when the humble balsamic is playing a part. Simply select a wine with good natural acidity to match the zip of the recipe.

Look to the Italians for inspiration: choose a Napa Valley Sangiovese or the Italian version usually labeled as Chianti. For a white, Pinot Grigio is just the ticket.

PROSCIUTTO-WRAPPED ASPARAGUS WITH MELON

I just love this combination! If serving as an appetizer, the asparagus can be finger food and the cantaloupe can be speared with toothpicks. For a starter course, fan the asparagus out on individual plates with the cantaloupe at the base of the asparagus. A fun alternative to a green salad!

> 1 cantaloupe
> 16 medium asparagus spears, cut to 5-inch lengths
> ¼ cup *Classic Dipping Oil with Balsamic*
> 4 long thin slices prosciutto
> ¼ cup grated Parmesan cheese

Preheat the oven to 450°F. Using a melon baller, scoop 16 balls out of the melon and set aside. Toss the asparagus with 2 tablespoons of the *Classic Dipping Oil with Balsamic.* Cut the prosciutto slices in half lengthwise, then cut each in half again so you have 16 long strips. Starting near the top of the asparagus spear right below the head, wrap each prosciutto strip around the asparagus in a spiral.

Place wrapped asparagus on a baking sheet and bake for 5 minutes. Remove from oven, sprinkle with Parmesan cheese, bake for another minute or two until cheese starts to melt. For a fun presentation, place the asparagus spears standing upright in tumblers sitting on salad plates and surround with the melon balls. Drizzle the melon balls with the remaining 2 tablespoons of the *Dipping Oil* and serve.

Serves 4 as an appetizer

GARDEN HERB DIPPING OIL WITH BALSAMIC

WE DO THE WORK FOR YOU BY COMBINING THE EXTRA-VIRGIN OLIVE OIL, HERBS, AND BALSAMIC TO MAKE A FLAVORFUL DIPPING OIL. APPETIZERS ARE A SNAP TO CREATE—JUST ADD FRESH VEGETABLES AND CRUSTY BREAD FOR DIPPING, OR DRIZZLE ON SKEWERS OF MEATS AND VEGETABLES BEFORE GRILLING.

GRILLED BREAD WITH TOMATOES & SHAVED MANCHEGO

1 loaf rustic-style Italian bread,
cut into 8 thick slices

Garden Herb Dipping Oil

4 medium vine-ripened tomatoes (the most flavorful you can find) cut into halves

Salt (preferably kosher or sea salt)

2 ounces Manchego cheese shaved (or Parmesan or Pecorino)

Prepare the grill. Place bread on grill, turn when you get some nice grill marks, then grill the other side. Transfer bread to a platter and drizzle with *Garden Herb Dipping Oil*.

Pass the platter around with a plate of the tomatoes, a crock of sea salt, and a bowl of cheese. Ask each guest to rub the cut side of the tomato vigorously over the bread, (set tomato aside or enjoy with the bread) sprinkle with salt and cheese and enjoy.

Serves 4 as an appetizer or starter course

28

MY FAVORITE BREAD SALAD

A yummy salad that can be thrown together in no time, this is best when vine-ripened tomatoes are available. Pugliese, a delicious Italian bread, is my favorite but any day-old bread works well.

½ loaf day-old bread, cut into 1-inch cubes

1 English cucumber, diced

8 ounces buffalo mozzarella, cut into ½-inch cubes

3 tomatoes, chopped

2 cups baby arugula

¼ cup *Garden Herb Dipping Oil*

Salt (preferably kosher or sea salt) and freshly ground pepper

Toss all the ingredients together in a large bowl. Add salt and pepper to taste.

Serves 4

WATERMELON-TOMATO SURPRISE

My friends Michael and Valarie came back from Spain and made a tomato gazpacho with a watermelon garnish and I loved it. This is a quick and easy appetizer along the same lines that is not only a great presentation but the flavors will surely surprise your guests.

¼ watermelon

18 cherry tomatoes or pear tomatoes

18 wooden skewers (small decorative toothpicks are great)

¼ cup *Garden Herb Dipping Oil*

Fresh edible flowers, chopped chives, or mint

Use either a small melon baller or half-teaspoon measuring spoon to scoop out 18 watermelon balls. Using a paring knife, cut a little off the bottom of each melon ball so they stand up. One at a time, skewer one tomato and then the watermelon, round side of the watermelon first. Stand up on serving plate. Continue with remaining tomatoes and watermelon. Drizzle the finished skewers with the *Garden Herb Dipping Oil* and then sprinkle with the flowers or herbs.

Serves 4 as an appetizer

PASTA PRIMAVERA

This is a perfect dish to make during the summer with all of the veggies coming out of the garden. Feel free to use any combination of vegetables—I especially like to include mushrooms in the group.

8 ounces dried orecchiette, penne, or fusilli

4 tablespoons *Garden Herb Dipping Oil*

1 pound fresh vegetables (broccoli, snow peas, asparagus, broccoli rabe, mushrooms, etc.)

¼ cup water

Salt (preferably kosher or sea salt)

3 ounces soft fresh goat cheese, crumbled

Grated Parmesan cheese, for serving

Prepare the pasta according to package instructions. Cut the vegetables into bite-size pieces. Heat 2 tablespoons of the *Garden Herb Dipping Oil* over medium-high heat in a large skillet. Add the vegetables, water, and a couple pinches of salt. Stir to coat the vegetables with oil, cover, and cook for about 5 minutes, shaking the pan frequently to prevent vegetables from sticking and adding more water, a tablespoon at a time if if they start to stick. The vegetables should be crisp but cooked through (cook longer if you like softer vegetables).

Stir the pasta and the remaining 2 tablespoons *Dipping Oil* into the vegetables. Add the goat cheese, stirring to incorporate but still leaving chunks of cheese. Serve with a sprinkle of grated Parmesan cheese.

Serves 4.

Wine Suggestions

This dipping oil is so versatile, it can be served with a variety of wines. A flavorful California Sauvignon Blanc or Napa Valley Viognier will lovingly match the savory herbs.

A rich, buttery Chardonnay will play nicely with the tomato bread, pasta, and bread salad. The Italian mainstays of Pinot Grigio and Sangiovese will work wonders with all the dishes.

You'll want to shake this really well before pouring so that you get a good mix of the olive oil, garlic, Parmesan cheese, and capers. For those trying to limit their bread intake, this dipping oil, while delicious with bread, is also fabulous tossed with shrimp or a variety of vegetables.

BRUSCHETTA WITH GARDEN TOMATOES & SHAVED PARMESAN

2 medium tomatoes, halved, seeds squeezed out, diced

2 tablespoons fresh julienned basil

2 tablespoons *Garlic Parmesan Dipping Oil with Capers*

Salt (preferably kosher or sea salt)

1 baguette, sliced on the diagonal

¼ cup shaved Parmesan cheese

Basil sprigs for garnish

Prepare the grill. In a small bowl, combine the tomatoes, basil, *Garlic Parmesan Dipping Oil,* and salt to taste. Grill the baguette slices on both sides. Spoon the tomato mixture onto the baguette slices and top with the cheese. Serve on a platter with additional basil sprigs tucked around.

Serves 4 as an appetizer

GARLIC SHRIMP FETTUCCINE

This is a fancy-sounding dish that is so easy and so delicious you can make it on Monday night!

8 ounces dried fettuccine

4 tablespoons *Garlic Parmesan Dipping Oil with Capers*

1 pound shrimp (21-25 count) peeled, tail left intact, and deveined

⅓ cup white wine or chicken or vegetable stock

Juice of 1 lemon

¼ cup chopped fresh basil or flat-leaf parsley

¼ cup grated Parmesan cheese, plus additional for serving

Salt (preferably kosher or sea salt) and freshly ground pepper

Prepare the pasta according to package instructions. Heat 2 tablespoons of the *Garlic Parmesan Dipping Oil with Capers* in a large skillet over medium heat. Add the shrimp and cook for 2-3 minutes, until the shrimp begin to turn pink and opaque. Add the wine and simmer for 3 minutes. Add the cooked pasta, lemon juice, herbs, and Parmesan cheese, and toss together to combine. Stir in the remaining 2 tablespoons *Dipping Oil,* season with salt and pepper to taste. Serve with additional Parmesan cheese sprinkled on top.

SUMMER PASTA WITH GRILLED CHICKEN & VEGETABLES

I love this dish and am inspired to make it when I have leftover grilled vegetables. Feel free to use your own combinations of veggies!

8 ounces orecchiette pasta or bow ties

1 large zucchini, cut in half lengthwise

1 ear of corn, husk removed

Olive oil

3 tablespoons *Mediterranean Medley Rub* (or season with salt and pepper)

1 large red bell pepper

1 pound boneless, skinless chicken breasts

2-3 tablespoons *Garlic Parmesan Dipping Oil with Capers*

Salt (preferably kosher or sea salt) and freshly ground pepper

½ cup grated Parmesan cheese

Prepare the grill. Prepare the pasta according to package instructions. Brush the zucchini and corn with olive oil and sprinkle with *Mediterranean Medley Rub.* Place on grill until grill marks appear; repeat on the other side. Cut the zucchini into 1-inch dice; cut kernels from corn using a sharp knife. Grill the red pepper until all sides are completely charred. Remove and place in a plastic bag to "sweat." When cool, remove the charred skin and cut pepper into 1-inch dice.

Sprinkle *Rub* on both sides of chicken breasts and grill for 5 to 7 minutes per side. Remove and cut into 1-inch dice.

Place the cooked pasta in a large bowl and toss with the *Garlic Parmesan Dipping Oil with Capers.* Add the vegetables, chicken, and salt and pepper to taste; mix well. Sprinkle with Parmesan cheese and serve, hot or at room temperature.

Serves 3-4

BRUSSELS SPROUTS WITH PROSCIUTTO

This is so tasty that even those who say they don't like Brussels sprouts become converts!

2 slices (about 1 ounce) prosciutto, cut into ¼-inch dice

4 tablespoons *Garlic Parmesan Dipping Oil with Capers*

1 pound Brussels sprouts, halved (smaller size preferred)

½ cup red onion, cut into ¼-inch dice

2 tablespoons water

Juice of 1 lemon

Freshly ground pepper

Heat a skillet over medium heat. Add the prosciutto and sauté until browned and crisp, about 2 minutes. Transfer to a small bowl. Add 2 tablespoons of the *Garlic Parmesan Dipping Oil with Capers* to the skillet, raise heat to medium-high, add the Brussels sprouts and onions and sauté, stirring frequently, for 2 minutes. Add the water, cover, and cook for 3 minutes, checking that the Brussels sprouts are not sticking; add more water if necessary. Stir in the prosciutto and remaining 2 tablespoons *Dipping Oil* and mix well. Finish by adding the lemon juice and a few pinches of pepper.

Serves 4 as a side dish

Berries

A PROLIFIC CROP OF
BERRIES AT OUR FRIEND
ROXANNA'S FARM TAUNTING
US AND THE BIRDS

CHAPTER 3

Fruit Balsamics

BLACKBERRY BALSAMIC VINEGAR WITH PEAR

Grilled Peaches with Blackberry Balsamic Sauce

Grilled Pork Tenderloin with Balsamic Reduction

Fennel, Pear & Gorgonzola Salad

Fresh Berries with Balsamic Cream

❈

FIG BALSAMIC VINEGAR WITH DATES

Grilled Stuffed Figs Wrapped in Prosciutto

Duck Breasts with Fig Sauce

Celery Salad with Dates

Lamb Kebabs with Apricots

❈

RASPBERRY BALSAMIC VINEGAR WITH LEMON

Cheese Plate

Balsamic-Glazed Chicken with Raspberries

Mixed Greens with Warm Goat Cheese Rounds & Raspberries

Caramelized Onion Tarts

JANE!

BLACKBERRY BALSAMIC VINEGAR WITH PEAR

❀❀❀❀❀❀❀❀❀❀❀❀❀❀❀❀❀❀

AGED BALSAMIC VINEGAR FROM MODENA, ITALY COMBINED WITH FRUIT IS SO FULL FLAVORED THAT ONCE YOU TRY IT YOU WILL BEGIN LOOKING FOR MORE WAYS TO USE IT. AT ITS SIMPLEST, JUST DRIZZLE ON BERRIES FOR A FLAVORFUL DESSERT WITHOUT THE GUILT. BUT DON'T STOP THERE, FLAVORED BALSAMICS ARE ALSO DELICIOUS IN SALAD DRESSINGS AND AS A REDUCTION SAUCE FOR GRILLED MEATS AND POULTRY.

❀

GRILLED PEACHES WITH BLACKBERRY BALSAMIC SAUCE

½ cup *Blackberry Balsamic Vinegar with Pear*

2 peaches, firm but ripe, halved & pitted

4 sprigs mint

½ cup crème fraîche

Bring the *Blackberry Balsamic Vinegar with Pear* to a boil in a 2-quart saucepan over high heat and cook until it is reduced to ¼ cup. Set aside.

Place peaches on a warm grill, approximately 250°F. Grill for about 10 minutes on each side, but don't let the fruit get soggy.

To serve, pour a pool of the balsamic reduction on each of four plates and top with a peach half and a dollop of crème fraîche. Garnish with mint. Or use whipped cream or vanilla ice cream in place of crème fraîche.

Serves 4

GRILLED PORK TENDERLOIN WITH BALSAMIC REDUCTION

This is a favorite of my sister Carla. She loves the fact that the balsamic reduction tastes like a complex French sauce, and is so easy to make. She doesn't tell anyone that it comes out of a bottle and you boil the heck out of it!

> 1 cup (8 ounces) *Blackberry Balsamic Vinegar with Pear*
> ¼ cup *Pork & Lamb Herb Rub* (or season with salt and freshly ground pepper)
> Two 12-14 ounce pork tenderloins
> Sour cream, for garnish
> Rosemary sprigs, for garnish

Prepare the grill. Bring the *Blackberry Balsamic Vinegar with Pear* to a boil in a 2-quart saucepan over high heat. Cook until reduced by half. While the sauce is reducing, place the rub in a ziplock bag, and add the pork, shaking a few times until pork is covered with *Pork & Lamb Herb Rub* (or season the pork with salt and pepper). Grill over a hot fire for about 5 minutes, turning a few times to develop a nice seared crust. Turn grill to low (if using charcoal, move pork to the side away from the direct heat) and cook, turning occasionally, for an additional 10-15 minutes. The pork should be light pink in the center. Transfer to a cutting board, cover with foil, and let rest for 5 minutes before slicing across the grain.

To serve, spoon about 2 tablespoons of the balsamic reduction onto each plate, top with pork slices, and garnish with a dollop of sour cream and a rosemary sprig.

Serves 4

FENNEL, PEAR & GORGONZOLA SALAD

Here is a great salad that can be served as a starter but is also perfect to serve alongside grilled poultry, meat, or fish on a hot summer night. Not only is it filled with all kinds of great flavors, it looks as good as it tastes.

2 fennel bulbs, shaved with a mandoline or large cheese grater

2 Bosc pears or your favorite pear, peeled, cored, and julienned

⅓ cup dried cranberries

⅓ cup crumbled Gorgonzola cheese

1 tablespoon extra-virgin olive oil

2 tablespoons *Blackberry Balsamic Vinegar with Pear*

Salt (preferably kosher or sea salt) and freshly ground pepper

In a medium bowl, combine the fennel, pears, cranberries, and Gorgonzola. In a separate bowl whisk together the oil and *Blackberry Balsamic Vinegar with Pear*. Pour over the fennel mixture, add salt and pepper to taste, and toss gently to combine.

Serves 4

Wine Suggestions

Sweet and tart, this vinegar delight when used in desserts will pair wonderfully with a red dessert wine such as port or late harvest Zinfandel.

But when used in a savory dish like the pork tenderloin or even the fennel salad it might just create a party at your table when you sip a Cabernet or Syrah with dinner!

FRESH BERRIES WITH BALSAMIC CREAM

The uses for balsamic vinegar seem to be endless. Adding the Blackberry Balsamic Vinegar with Pear *to the whipped cream makes it almost a soft mocha color and gives it a flavor that people will have a hard time deciphering. Delicious!*

¾ cup *Blackberry Balsamic Vinegar with Pear*

½ pint whipping cream

2-4 tablespoons granulated sugar

4 cups fresh berries: strawberries, blueberries, blackberries, raspberries, or a combination

2-3 tablespoons brown sugar

Place the *Blackberry Balsamic Vinegar with Pear* in a small saucepan over medium heat. Simmer until the sauce is reduced to ¼ cup, stirring occasionally. Remove from heat and allow to cool. Whip the cream, adding granulated sugar to taste. Fold the cooled balsamic reduction into the whipped cream, mixing well. Spoon berries into individual serving bowls, and top with the whipped cream and a little brown sugar.

Serves 4

FIGS, DATES AND BALSAMIC VINEGAR ARE A COMBINATION MADE IN HEAVEN! THIS FLAVOR-PACKED JEWEL CAN BE USED TO CREATE A SIMPLE YET ELEGANT DRESSING WHEN COMBINED WITH EXTRA-VIRGIN OLIVE OIL FOR ARUGULA OR SPINACH SALADS. LAMB, PORK, AND DUCK ARE DELICIOUS DRIZZLED WITH THIS BALSAMIC VINEGAR AS WELL.

❈

GRILLED STUFFED FIGS WRAPPED IN PROSCIUTTO

12 medium fresh figs, stems cut off

3 ounces Gorgonzola cheese, cut into 12 pieces

3-4 slices prosciutto, cut into 12 strips (about 1 inch wide and 6 inches long)

Fig Balsamic Vinegar with Dates, for drizzling

Prepare the grill. Slit the figs into quarters starting at top but don't cut through the bottom. Stuff a piece of cheese into the center of each fig, pinching the top of the fig together to enclose the cheese. Wrap each fig with a piece of prosciutto.

Place the figs on the grill bottom side down, turning to grill the sides as the prosciutto begins to brown. Remove the figs from the grill when the prosciutto is browned all around and the figs are soft, about 5 minutes. Serve immediately with a drizzle of *Fig Balsamic Vinegar with Dates*.

Serves 4-6 as an appetizer

38

DUCK BREASTS WITH FIG SAUCE

Duck is my first choice for this dish, but if you can't get it, you can use boneless chicken thighs. But I highly recommend "hunting" for the duck!

4 duck breast halves, skin on

2 teaspoons salt, (preferably kosher or sea salt)

1 cup *Fig Balsamic Vinegar with Dates*

1 cup dry white wine

2 tablespoons butter

Using a sharp knife, score the duck skin diagonally, about ½-inch apart. Heat a large heavy skillet over high heat. When hot, sprinkle the bottom of the pan with salt. Add the duck breasts, skin side down; reduce heat to medium-high. Cook 4 to 5 minutes per side, depending on their thickness. Transfer duck to a plate, cover with foil, and allow to rest for 10 minutes.

Combine the *Fig Balsamic Vinegar with Dates* and wine in a medium saucepan over high heat. Bring to a boil; reduce heat to medium. Simmer, stirring occasionally, until the mixture is reduced by half. Add the butter and whisk until completely incorporated.

To serve, slice the duck breasts along the scored lines, arrange on individual plates, and drizzle with the fig reduction.

Serves 4

CELERY SALAD WITH DATES

The Martini House restaurant in St. Helena inspired this salad. Who knew celery could taste and look so good?

2 tablespoons *Fig Balsamic Vinegar with Dates*

2 tablespoons extra-virgin olive oil

2 tablespoons buttermilk

3-4 stalks celery, strings removed and sliced thinly on the diagonal, about 3 cups

½ cup diced dates

⅓ cup coarsely chopped walnuts, toasted

2 tablespoons chopped fresh tarragon leaves or flat-leaf parsley

Salt (preferably kosher or sea salt) and freshly ground pepper

For the dressing, whisk together the *Fig Balsamic Vinegar with Dates*, olive oil, and buttermilk and set aside. In another bowl, combine the celery, dates, walnuts, and tarragon and toss with the dressing (using less dressing if you like your salad lightly dressed). Season with salt and pepper to taste.

Serves 4 as a side dish

LAMB KEBABS WITH APRICOTS

I wanted these skewers to have more than just lamb and veggies. Our creative director and good friend Julia told me about the bread and apricot combination and boy was she right on!

½ loaf sourdough bread, cut into thick slices

2 tablespoons olive oil

¼ cup *Fig Balsamic Vinegar with Dates*, plus more for drizzling

Salt (preferably kosher or sea salt) and freshly ground pepper

1½ pounds boneless leg of lamb cut into 1½-inch cubes

½ large red onion cut into 1½-inch pieces

24 dried apricots or 12 fresh apricots halved, or 24 large grapes

8 wood skewers soaked in water for 30 minutes

Prepare the grill. Grill the bread slices, then cut them into 1½-inch pieces (24 cubes).

In a large bowl, whisk together the olive oil, ¼ cup *Fig Balsamic Vinegar with Dates*, and a pinch of salt and pepper. Add the lamb, onion, and apricots, toss to coat well. Thread the skewers with the lamb, onion, apricots, and bread, alternating ingredients. Grill the kebabs, turning about every 3-4 minutes until the meat is cooked to your liking; 2-3 minutes per side will be about medium rare. Transfer the kebabs to a platter, drizzle with additional *Balsamic Vinegar,* and serve with couscous.

Serves 4

Wine Suggestions

The fig teams with sweet dates and the tang of balsamic to give you a fine set of wine-friendly flavors.

Pair the duck with a rich, black cherry Russian River Valley Pinot Noir. The lamb kebabs and a hearty Syrah (or Shiraz) are made for each other, while the figs are best with a fruity sparkling wine like a Asti Spumante or Prosecco from Italy.

RASPBERRY BALSAMIC VINEGAR WITH LEMON

BALSAMIC VINEGAR COMBINED WITH RIPE RASPBERRY AND CITRUSY LEMON IS A BRIGHT-FLAVORED PANTRY STAPLE THAT IS EQUALLY DELICIOUS WITH SAVORY AND SWEET DISHES. PAN-ROASTED CHICKEN BECOMES A GORGEOUS ENTRÉE WITH THE ADDITION OF THIS BALSAMIC THAT IS SIMPLE BUT ELEGANT ENOUGH FOR A SPECIAL DINNER.

CHEESE PLATE

One 4-ounce wedge tangy goat cheese

One 4-ounce wedge ripe blue cheese

One 4-ounce wedge aged Jack cheese

½ cup toasted nuts (walnuts, almonds, or pistachios)

4 ounces dried pears or seasonal fresh fruit

Raspberry Balsamic Vinegar with Lemon

Slices of walnut bread

Arrange the cheese, nuts, pears, and bread on a platter. If you have access to fresh fig leaves, line the platter with them before arranging the ingredients. Serve with a small pitcher of *Raspberry Balsamic Vinegar with Lemon* for drizzling over the cheese.

Serves 4 as an appetizer or cheese course

BALSAMIC-GLAZED CHICKEN WITH RASPBERRIES

I love to serve this dish on Valentine's Day because it seems like a natural with the raspberries. But it's so good I get requests for it all year round. Feel free to add a dollop of crème fraîche.

2 tablespoons butter

4 boneless, skinless chicken breast halves (about 2 pounds)

Salt (preferably kosher or sea salt) and freshly ground pepper

2 shallots, finely minced

½ cup *Raspberry Balsamic Vinegar with Lemon*

3 tablespoons chicken stock

½ pint fresh raspberries or thawed frozen berries

2 tablespoons fresh thyme leaves, plus additional thyme sprigs for garnish

Melt the butter in a large skillet over medium-high heat. Season the chicken with salt and pepper to taste. Add to skillet and cook 3 minutes per side until golden. Transfer to a plate and cover with foil.

Add the shallots to the skillet, reduce heat to medium, cover, and cook until softened, about 5 minutes. Add the *Raspberry Balsamic Vinegar with Lemon*, raise the heat, and cook for 1 minute, reducing the vinegar to a syrup. Whisk in the stock and cook 1 minute more.

Return the chicken breasts to the pan, spoon the sauce over them, cover, and simmer 5 minutes. Add the raspberries and thyme; swirl the pan to coat the raspberries. Serve the chicken sliced on the diagonal on warm plates with the sauce spooned on top. Garnish with a sprig of thyme.

Serves 4

MIXED GREENS WITH WARM GOAT CHEESE ROUNDS & RASPBERRIES

I recently had this salad at Bouchon (one of Thomas Keller's restaurants in Yountville) but they didn't have the raspberries. So if you don't have them, don't hesitate to make the salad. It is still delicious!

1 cup fresh bread crumbs made from day-old bread, processed fine in a blender

2 tablespoons chopped fresh thyme leaves

¼ teaspoon salt (preferably kosher or sea salt)

¼ teaspoon freshly ground pepper

1 egg, beaten

One 8-ounce log fresh goat cheese, cut into 8 rounds

2 tablespoons *Raspberry Balsamic Vinegar with Lemon*

2 tablespoons extra-virgin olive oil

6 cups mixed salad greens

½ pint raspberries

Prepare the goat cheese rounds by mixing the breadcrumbs, thyme, salt, and pepper in a shallow bowl. Place the egg in another shallow bowl. Dip each round into the egg and then press into the breadcrumbs, coating all sides. Heat a large skillet with a little olive oil over medium heat, add the rounds and cook until browned and crisp, about 1½-2 minutes per side. Keep warm.

Prepare dressing by whisking together the *Raspberry Balsamic Vinegar with Lemon* and oil. Place the greens in a large bowl, toss with the dressing, and divide among four plates. Top each salad with a sprinkle of raspberries, and 2 goat cheese rounds.

Serves 4

CARAMELIZED ONION TARTS

This is so easy and delicious you will be proud to serve it for any occasion. You can make this for Sunday brunch, Friday evening wine time, or during the week as an entrée. Serve it with a mixed green salad or bowl of soup and you'll be quite the gourmet.

3 tablespoons olive oil

2 large sweet onions, sliced thin

2 teaspoons salt (preferably kosher or sea salt)

½ cup *Raspberry Balsamic Vinegar with Lemon*

1 sheet frozen puff pastry, thawed

3 ounces Gruyère cheese, shaved

Preheat the oven to 450°F. Heat the olive oil in a large skillet over medium-high heat. Add the onions and salt and toss until they are coated with the oil. Cover and cook for 7 minutes, checking to make sure that they are not sticking to the bottom of the pan. Uncover and add the *Raspberry Balsamic Vinegar with Lemon* and mix well. Reduce the heat to low and cook for 40 minutes, uncovered.

While the onions are cooking, cut the puff pastry in half lengthwise. Roll each half out to about ⅛-inch thick. Place pastry halves on a baking sheet and fold the edges over about ¼ inch all around and press with the tines of a fork. Brush the edges with egg white (or water). Once the onions are caramelized, divide them evenly between the tarts. Top with the cheese and bake for 12-15 minutes, until golden brown. Let the tarts cool a couple of minutes before cutting into squares. Serve on a platter with sprigs of rosemary.

Serves 4 as a light entrée or 6 as an appetizer

Wine Suggestions

There is a wine to please everyone here—whether red or white!

Look for fresh young whites with crisp acidity such as Chardonay, Pinot Gris/Pinot Grigio, and Sauvignon Blanc to balance the wonderful tartness of this vinegar.

The succulent raspberry flavors will highlight the berry notes of lighter-bodied, berry-scented reds such as Pinot Noir, Sangiovese or Zinfandel.

CHAPTER 4

Marinades and Sauces

APPLE CHIPOTLE FINISHING SAUCE

Smoky Apple-Turkey Sandwich

Grilled Pork Chops with Chipotle Apples

Apple, White Cheddar & Chicken Tostadas

Chipotle-Spiced Sweet Potato Puree

BAJA MARINADE WITH CHILES & LIME

Baja Chicken Salad

Steamed Halibut Packets

Flank Steak Fajitas

Rice Salad with Shrimp & Avocado

CHIMI CHURRI MARINADE

Grilled Flank Steak Argentina

Grilled Chicken with Tropical Salsa

Scallop Ceviche

Swordfish Veracruzana

HERB MARINADE WITH MERLOT

Red-Wine-Marinated Tri-Tip Sirloin

Wine-Infused Leg of Lamb

Baked Mushrooms with Merlot

Chicken Packets with Artichokes & Mushrooms

KOREAN SOY GINGER MARINADE

Marinated Seafood

Garden Vegetable Stir-Fry

Rolling Lettuce Cups

Ginger-Soy Hanger Steak

PAN-ASIAN DIPPING SAUCE & DRESSING

Asian Broccoli Slaw

Seared Ahi Tuna Salad

Asian Noodles

Shrimp & Vegetable Summer Rolls

SHANGHAI TANGERINE SESAME MARINADE

Asian Appetizers

Shanghai Pizza

Sesame Swordfish Skewers with Dipping Sauce

Soba Noodles with Chicken & Vegetables

YUCATAN THREE CHILES & CITRUS MARINADE

Chicken Enchiladas

Chicken Tortilla Soup

Yucatan Pulled-Pork Sandwiches

Chile & Citrus Crab Cocktail

Sweetness from the apples and the smoky heat from the chipotle chiles combine in a sauce full of flavor. Perfect for pork chops and tenderloin, or turkey, chicken, and Cornish game hens. Equally delicious with sweet potatoes and winter squashes.

Smoky Apple-Turkey Sandwich

8 ounces whipped cream cheese

½ cup *Apple Chipotle Finishing Sauce*

Sliced bread, your choice

Alfalfa sprouts

Sliced turkey breast meat

1 tart apple (Pippin or Granny Smith), cut into ¼-inch slices

In a medium bowl, mix the cream cheese and the *Apple Chipotle Finishing Sauce* thoroughly. Spread the mixture generously on 2 slices of bread. Add the alfalfa sprouts to one side and then cover with turkey and apple slices. Top with other slice of bread and press sandwich down slightly before cutting in half.

Makes enough spread for 4 sandwiches

GRILLED PORK CHOPS WITH CHIPOTLE APPLES

When paired with apples, pork "the other white meat", is a match made in heaven (hog heaven that is). The key ingredient here is the smoky, sweet glaze brushed on the chops as they are pulled off the grill.

Four 8–10 ounce loin pork chops, bone in, or center-cut boneless pork loin

Salt (preferably kosher or sea salt) and freshly ground pepper

¼ cup plus 2 tablespoons *Apple Chipotle Finishing Sauce*

1 tablespoon olive oil

1 large red onion, halved and cut into ¼-inch-thick half-moons

4 large tart green apples (Granny Smith or Pippin), peeled and cut into ¼-inch-thick wedges

1 tablespoon minced fresh sage leaves

Prepare the grill. Season the pork chops on both sides with salt and pepper and place on grill. Depending on the heat of the grill and thickness of chops, it will take 4-5 minutes per side. Brush each side with the *Apple Chipotle Finishing Sauce* as you remove them from the grill. Check for doneness by making a small cut in the center of the chop, which should be barely pink.

Heat the oil in a large skillet over medium-high heat. Add the onions, a couple of pinches of salt and grindings of black pepper, cover, and cook until they begin to soften, about 5 minutes. Add the apples and sage and cook about 3 minutes, stirring frequently. The apples will soften and may break apart; that's okay, this is a rustic preparation. Add the remaining *Finishing Sauce*; stir to combine, and cook another 1-2 minutes. Serve as a side with the pork chops, topped with a sprig of sage.

Serves 4

APPLE, WHITE CHEDDAR & CHICKEN TOSTADAS

This is a yummy twist on a tostada, combining apples and chicken tossed with a smoky sauce that has a hint of sweet and a little kick of heat. White cheddar is a perfect cheese to top it off. You can also make these with purchased tostada shells for a light entrée, or with round flat tortilla chips for mini tostada appetizers.

1 cup shredded cooked chicken

1 large tart apple (Granny Smith or Pippin), cored and cut into ¼-inch dice

6 tablespoons (or more) *Apple Chipotle Finishing Sauce*

2 flour tortillas, burrito size

⅔ cup shredded white cheddar (4 ounces) or your favorite melting cheese

2 green onions (white and green parts) sliced thin on the diagonal

Preheat the oven to broil. Stir together the chicken, apples, and *Apple Chipotle Finishing Sauce*. Place the tortillas on a large foil-lined baking sheet and bake for about 1 minute until they begin to brown in spots. Turn and bake the other side until the tortillas are crisp, about 1 minute more. Divide the chicken mixture between the tortillas, top with the cheese and green onions. Broil for 3-4 minutes (watch carefully) until cheese is melted and edges are browning. Cut into wedges and serve immediately.

Serves 4 as an appetizer, or 2 as a light entrée

CHIPOTLE-SPICED SWEET POTATO PUREE

What a great combination of ingredients—a little spice, a little sweet, and a little earthiness. Of course Thanksgiving turkey comes to mind, but also think roast pork, chicken, or beef any time of the year.

2-3 sweet potatoes (2 pounds), peeled and cut into 2-inch cubes

3 tablespoons butter

2 tablespoons brown sugar

½ cup (or more) *Apple Chipotle Finishing Sauce*

Salt (preferably kosher or sea salt)

Bring a large pot of lightly salted water to a boil over high heat. Add the sweet potatoes and cook until tender, about 10 minutes. Drain the potatoes, return to the pan, and place over low heat, shaking a few times to remove the moisture, 10-15 seconds. Place the potatoes in the bowl of an electric mixer fitted with the paddle attachment and add the butter, brown sugar, *Apple Chipotle Finishing Sauce,* and salt to taste, and beat until smooth. Serve immediately or keep warm by placing mixing bowl over a pot of barely simmering water.

Variation: You can substitute Russet potatoes for a more savory flavor, or combine half sweet potatoes and half Russets for a little less sweet flavor.

Serves 4 as a side dish

Wine Suggestions

For any of these dishes, a vibrant Riesling or spicy Gewürztraminer will be perfect to match the zesty flavors and tickle of heat from the Finishing Sauce. The wines can be dry or even a little sweet.

A soft and yummy red such as Gamay or Pinot Noir will tantalize the senses just as well.

BAJA MARINADE WITH CHILES & LIME

CHILES, LIME, AND CILANTRO ARE REMINISCENT OF FLAVORS FROM SOUTH OF THE BORDER. WHILE THIS IS A TASTY MARINADE FOR FISH, PORK, AND CHICKEN, I EVEN LIKE IT WITH STEAK. USE IN FISH TACOS OR AS A DIPPING SAUCE FOR PRAWNS OR GRILLED SKEWERS.

BAJA CHICKEN SALAD

1 pound chicken tenders

1 cup *Baja Marinade with Chiles & Lime*

1 tablespoon sugar

Approximately 4 to 5 cups chopped romaine lettuce or mixed baby greens

1 avocado, sliced

1 orange, cut off pith and cut into segments

¼ cup chopped cilantro leaves

In a ziplock bag, combine the chicken and ½ cup of the *Baja Marinade with Chiles & Lime* and refrigerate 1 hour. In a small bowl, stir together the remaining ½ cup of *Baja Marinade* and the sugar, set aside.

Cook the chicken either on the grill or in a sauté pan; about 3 minutes per side.

Mix the greens with some of the reserved dressing and divide among four plates. Top the greens with chicken, avocado, and oranges. Drizzle the dressing over the top and sprinkle with cilantro.

Serves 4

48

STEAMED HALIBUT PACKETS

My butcher Cathy suggested using lettuce leaves for this dish if I couldn't find banana leaves. I tried it and it worked great! This dish makes me want to eat fish more often.

Four 4-ounce halibut fillets

1 cup *Baja Marinade with Chiles & Lime*

8 large lettuce leaves (butter lettuce or romaine work well), or banana leaves cut into 12-inch squares

4 slices tomato

2 limes, halved

½ red onion, diced

3 tablespoons chopped cilantro leaves

½ jalapeño, seeds and ribs removed, minced

1 avocado, diced

Salt (preferably kosher or sea salt)

In a ziplock bag, combine the fish and *Baja Marinade with Chiles & Lime* and refrigerate for at least 2 hours. To assemble packets, take two lettuce leaves stem ends overlapping. Set fish in the middle, place a tomato slice on top, squeeze a half lime over the tomato, and fold the lettuce leaves over the fish to meet in the center, secure with a toothpick. Repeat with remaining fillets (or use banana leaves pulled up and tied with kitchen string as shown in photo).

Prepare a steamer and bring the water to a boil. Place the fish packets in the steamer, cover, and steam for about 8-10 minutes depending on the thickness of the fish.

While the fish is cooking, in a small bowl, stir together the onion, cilantro, jalapeño, avocado, and a pinch of salt for the garnish. To serve, discard lettuce leaves and top the fish with garnish.

Serves 4

FLANK STEAK FAJITAS

This is a one-dish meal that both adults and kids will rave about. Feel free to throw in corn, black beans, or whatever you like. Save any leftovers for lunch the next day. Muy bueno!

> 1½ pounds flank steak, sliced into thin strips
>
> ¾ cup *Baja Marinade with Chiles & Lime*
>
> 1 tablespoon olive oil
>
> 1 large red bell pepper, seeds and ribs removed, cut into thin strips
>
> ½ medium red onion cut into ½-inch-wide wedges
>
> 1 avocado, sliced
>
> 8 flour tortillas

In a ziplock bag, combine the beef strips and *Baja Marinade with Chiles & Lime* and refrigerate for 1 hour. In a large skillet, heat the oil over medium-high heat. Add the beef strips and sauté, stirring occasionally until beef is lightly browned, about 2 minutes. Transfer the beef to a bowl and cover with foil.

Reduce heat to medium, add the peppers and onions to the hot pan and sauté until softened and onions are browning, stirring occasionally, about 5-7 minutes (add a little water to prevent sticking). Increase the heat to high and add the beef back to the pan with the peppers and onions. Add a little more *Marinade* to the pan, stirring to loosen the browned bits. Immediately transfer the beef mixture to the warm platter. Garnish with avocado and serve with warm flour tortillas.

Serves 4

Wine Suggestions

Zesty lime and mild chiles are a great combination flavorwise. For a refreshing summery combo, try whites like Pinot Grigio or Sauvignon Blanc; both will match the crisp herbal flavors in the chicken and halibut recipes.

The rice salad will be best with a dry Riesling while the flank steak fajitas calls for a light-to-medium-bodied Merlot.

RICE SALAD WITH SHRIMP & AVOCADO

Not your typical rice salad for sure. If you want to take it a step further, stuff the salad into roasted poblano chiles for a healthy chile relleno! Top with a little cheese and put in the oven until cheese melts and rice is heated all the way through.

> 5 cups cooked long-grain rice (basmati or jasmine)
>
> 1 large red bell pepper, seeded and cut into ¼-inch dice
>
> 4 ounces feta cheese
>
> ¼ cup finely chopped fresh mint leaves
>
> 6 tablespoons *Baja Marinade with Chiles & Lime*
>
> 2 tablespoons olive oil
>
> 2 tablespoons water
>
> Juice of 1 lime
>
> 1 pound cooked and peeled shrimp (31-40 count)
>
> 2 ripe avocados, cut into ½-inch cubes

In a large bowl, combine the cooled rice, red pepper, feta, and mint. For the dressing, in a small bowl whisk together the *Baja Marinade with Chiles & Lime*, oil, water, and lime juice. Stir the dressing and the shrimp into the rice mixture and serve topped with the avocado. (The salad can be made up to 4 hours ahead, but wait to add the avocado until ready to serve.)

Serves 6 as a side dish or 2-3 as an entrée

CHIMI CHURRI IS AN ARGENTINEAN TABLE CONDIMENT THAT THE LOCALS USE EVERY DAY. IT HAS THE FLAVORS OF THE SOUTH WITH OREGANO, CILANTRO, CHILES, AND VINEGAR. USE AS A MARINADE FOR FISH, STEAKS, PORK, AND CHICKEN, OR AS A SALSA ON BURRITOS OR TACOS, EVEN EGGS.

GRILLED FLANK STEAK ARGENTINA

1½ pounds flank steak

1⅓ cups *Chimi Churri Marinade*

Chopped green onions or fresh herbs, for garnish

Combine the flank steak and 1 cup of the *Chimi Churri Marinade* in a ziplock bag and marinate at least 2 hours in the refrigerator. Remove the steak from the refrigerator 20-30 minutes before you plan to start grilling

Prepare the grill. Grill the meat directly over the heat for about 5 minutes per side, brushing with more *Marinade* before turning it. Remove the steak from the grill, cover with foil, and let rest for 5 minutes. Slice the steak across the grain and serve topped with the remaining *Marinade* and a sprinkling of the green onions or fresh herbs.

Serves 4

GRILLED CHICKEN WITH TROPICAL SALSA

Chicken with fruit salsa is so refreshing on a hot summer night. I like a little heat with the fruit, so if you do too, add a chopped jalapeño or serrano to the salsa.

> 6–8 boneless, skinless chicken breast halves
>
> 1¼ cups *Chimi Churri Marinade*
>
> 1 cup diced oranges
>
> 1 cup diced pineapple
>
> ½ cup diced red onion
>
> ¼ cup finely chopped cilantro leaves
>
> 3 limes: 1 squeezed for juice, 2 peeled and diced
>
> Salt (preferably kosher or sea salt)

In a ziplock bag, combine the chicken breasts and the *Chimi Churri Marinade* and refrigerate overnight.

To make the salsa: at least 40 minutes before serving combine the fruit, onion, and cilantro in a nonreactive bowl and mix well. Add lime juice and salt to taste and mix again. Stir every 10 minutes or so to allow juices to mix.

Prepare the grill. Grill the chicken over medium heat until cooked through, usually 5-6 minutes per side. Serve the chicken with a spoonful of salsa over the top.

Scallop Ceviche

I first tasted this dish while sitting on a beach in Rosarita Beach in Baja California and now every time I make it, I can almost smell the ocean!

1 pound bay scallops (or combine half scallops and half baby shrimp, or use all baby shrimp)

½ cup *Chimi Churri Marinade* (plus more if needed to cover scallops)

Juice of 2 limes

Salt (preferably kosher or sea salt) and freshly ground pepper

½ jalapeño, seeds and ribs removed, finely diced

1 cup halved cherry tomatoes

¼ cup minced red onion

1 avocado, diced

¼ cup chopped cilantro leaves, plus sprigs for garnish

Tortilla chips

In a medium nonreactive bowl, combine the scallops, *Chimi Churri Marinade*, and lime juice. Cover and refrigerate for 3 hours or until the scallops are firm and opaque all the way through. Add salt and pepper to taste, jalapeño, tomatoes, onion, and avocado, and toss well. Spoon the ceviche into individual serving dishes (martini glasses are festive), top with cilantro sprigs, and pass a basket of chips.

Note: If you choose to use just the baby shrimp—which will be cooked—you can eliminate the refrigeration process and proceed with recipe as indicated after the initial step.

Serves 4 as a starter course

Swordfish Veracruzana

This dish makes for a striking presentation with the white fish topped by the colorful and tasty olive and orange salsa. Serve with rice to soak up the juices.

½ cup plus 2 tablespoons *Chimi Churri Marinade*

1½ pounds swordfish, cut into 4 steaks

Salt (preferably kosher or sea salt) and freshly ground pepper

2 oranges, pith removed, cut into segments, and coarsely chopped

16 green olives, pitted and coarsely chopped

1 scallion (white and green parts), thinly sliced on the diagonal

¼ cup coarsely chopped cilantro leaves

Preheat the oven to 400°F. Oil a baking pan large enough to hold the fish in a single layer. Spoon ¼ cup of the *Chimi Churri Marinade* into the bottom of the pan. Season each fish steak with salt and pepper and place in the pan. Pour ¼ cup of the *Marinade* over the fish and place in the oven. Bake for 10 to 15 minutes until cooked through.

While the fish is cooking, prepare the salsa. In a small bowl, combine the remaining 2 tablespoons of the *Marinade*, oranges, olives, scallions, and cilantro. To serve, top each swordfish steak with a spoonful of the salsa and juices from the baking pan.

Variation: For an even easier preparation, replace the salsa ingredients with *Green Olive with Roasted Tomatoes Tapenade*.

Serves 4

Wine Suggestions

The green herbal notes in Chimi Churri are just right with crisp whites like Sauvignon Blanc or light-to-medium-bodied reds like Grenache or Pinot Noir.

However, the big meaty flavor of flank steak is ideal with a big Cabernet or Shiraz. Light and delicate, the scallop ceviche is matched by Sauvignon Blanc but it takes a tropical, oaky Chardonnay to handle the grilled chicken or swordfish.

THIS MARINADE IS LOADED WITH ALL KINDS OF CHUNKY, YUMMY HERBS, GARLIC, AND LOTS OF MERLOT! OF COURSE WITH MERLOT AS AN INGREDIENT IT IS FABULOUS FOR BEEF, LAMB, AND PORK, BUT I LOVE IT WITH CHICKEN AS WELL. THE LONGER YOU MARINATE, THE MORE THE FLAVORS COME OUT.

RED-WINE-MARINATED TRI-TIP SIRLOIN

1½-2 pounds tri-tip sirloin steak (also called bottom sirloin butt or triangle roast), trimmed of fat

1 cup *Herb Marinade with Merlot*

Salt (preferably kosher or sea salt) and freshly ground pepper

In a ziplock bag, combine the tri-tip and *Herb Marinade with Merlot* (shake well) and shake to coat the meat. Refrigerate for 4 hours or up to 48 hours, turning the bag every couple of hours.

Prepare the grill. Remove the tri-tip from the bag and season with salt and pepper. Grill at a temperature of 375°-400°F for about 20 minutes, turn and grill until the internal temperature reaches 140°F for medium rare. Remove from grill, cover with foil, and let rest for 10 minutes. Slice and serve with *Mediterranean Roasted Potatoes* (see page 88).

Serves 4-6

WINE-INFUSED LEG OF LAMB

My mother, and also long time good friend Eve would ask for this dish whenever they would visit. The next day, it makes the best sandwich or a lovely lamb salad with blue cheese. Ask your butcher to butterfly the leg of lamb for you.

One 4-5 pound boneless leg of lamb, butterflied

2 cups *Herb Marinade with Merlot*

One 750 ml bottle dry red wine or 32 ounces chicken or vegetable stock

Salt (preferably kosher or sea salt) and freshly ground pepper

Place the lamb in a large baking dish or bowl (or in a medium-size plastic kitchen trash bag.) Shake up the *Herb Marinade with Merlot* and pour over the lamb. If using a baking dish, cover with plastic wrap (or tie up the plastic bag.) Refrigerate for 4 hours or up to 48 hours, turning the meat every couple of hours.

Preheat the oven to 425°F. Place the lamb in a roasting pan and pour in the wine. Cook for 20 minutes, then reduce heat to 350°F (you may want to add a little more liquid if needed). Cook to the desired temperature. Start checking the temperature after 30 minutes, medium rare is equivalent to 140°F. Remove from oven, cover with foil, and let rest for 20 minutes. Slice and serve.

Serves 4-6

BAKED MUSHROOMS WITH MERLOT

Red wine and mushrooms are such a fabulous combination. Not your typical use for a marinade but I think you will be pleased!

> 1 pound assorted fresh mushrooms (such as chanterelles, shiitake, cremini, porcini, or hedgehogs), cut into 1-inch pieces
>
> ¼ cup plus 1 tablespoon *Herb Marinade with Merlot*
>
> Salt (preferably kosher or sea salt) and freshly ground pepper
>
> ¼ cup grated Parmesan cheese
>
> 3 tablespoons crushed toasted bread crumbs
>
> 1 loaf crusty bread (sourdough baguette), sliced on the diagonal and toasted or grilled

Preheat the oven to 350°F. Place the mushrooms in a baking pan large enough to hold them in a 1-inch layer. Mix ¼ cup of the *Herb Marinade with Merlot* with the mushrooms and spread them out evenly in the pan. Sprinkle the mushrooms with a couple pinches of salt and pepper, the Parmesan cheese, and breadcrumbs. Drizzle with the remaining 1 tablespoon of the *Marinade*. Bake until the mushrooms start to turn a golden brown, about 15-20 minutes. Serve with the baguette slices.

Serves 4-6 as an appetizer or as a side dish

Wine Suggestions

This is easy; serve a Merlot in spite of what Miles (of Sideways movie fame) says! A full-bodied Napa Valley Merlot with supple tannins will harmonize beautifully with all of these recipes.

You could also substitute a Cabernet Sauvignon (one that's not too tannic), or for the poultry dish choose a dry, flavorsome Napa Valley Sauvignon Blanc that packs a punch of herbs.

CHICKEN PACKETS WITH ARTICHOKES & MUSHROOMS

Your guests will think you spent all day making this pretty dish, and it is really easy. If you don't like artichoke hearts or olives, leave them out. Just add more mushrooms.

> 4 sheets 12 x 16-inch parchment paper (or aluminum foil)
>
> 4 boneless, skinless chicken breast halves (about 8 ounces each)
>
> Salt (preferably kosher or sea salt) and freshly ground pepper
>
> ¼ cup *Herb Marinade with Merlot*
>
> 16 cremini (brown) mushrooms, medium size, sliced ¼-inch thick
>
> One 6-ounce jar marinated artichoke hearts, drained and cut lengthwise into ¼-inch slices
>
> 16 kalamata olives, pitted and halved
>
> 1 clove garlic, minced

Preheat the oven to 350°F. Fold each sheet of parchment in half lengthwise and cut a fat half-heart shape. When unfolded you will have a fat heart shape. Season chicken breasts with salt and pepper. Place each breast on one half of the parchment heart and close to the fold. Spoon 1 tablespoon of the *Herb Marinade with Merlot* over each breast, top with ¼ of the mushrooms, artichokes, olives, and garlic. Fold the parchment over the chicken and starting at one edge fold the paper over twice, making pleats all the way around to enclose the chicken tightly. (Note: there should be about 1 inch of space between the contents of the package and the edge of the folded paper.)

Place the packets on a large baking sheet and bake for 30 minutes. To serve, transfer each packet to a plate. Let your dinner guests inhale the aromas when you cut open their packet for them as you serve.

Serves 4

KOREAN SOY GINGER MARINADE

All of those Asian flavors that we love—ginger, soy, and sesame are married together in this marinade that can also be used in stir-fries. You'll find this to be a must-have staple in your pantry.

MARINATED SEAFOOD

Seafood (shrimp, scallops, halibut, sea bass, salmon, swordfish, tuna, cod, etc.)

Korean Soy Ginger Marinade

Place your seafood in a ziplock bag with enough *Korean Soy Ginger Marinade* to coat well. Close bag and marinate for 30 minutes. Remove the seafood from marinade and grill, pan sear, oven roast, or broil. Brush more *Marinade* on in the last minute of cooking. Serve with rice and Asian vegetables.

GARDEN VEGETABLE STIR-FRY

Here's a great dish to make sure you eat your veggies! Jam-packed with flavor, this is the type of recipe where you can add or subtract any of the vegetables to make it different each time. Serve with a bowl of steamed rice or noodles.

2 tablespoons peanut or canola oil

1 large carrot, peeled and cut on the diagonal into ⅛-inch pieces

1 cup medium shiitake mushrooms, stemmed and quartered

12 asparagus spears cut on the diagonal into 1-inch pieces

1 large red bell pepper, seeded and cut into ¼-inch-wide strips

1 cup Chinese pea pods

2 scallions (white and green parts) cut on the diagonal into ½-inch pieces

½ cup *Korean Soy Ginger Marinade*

½ cup coarsely chopped toasted walnuts (optional)

Heat the oil in a large skillet or wok over medium-high heat. Add the carrots and cook for 1 minute. Constantly stirring after each addition to the pan, add the mushrooms and cook for 1 minute. Add the asparagus, red peppers, and pea pods and cook for 2 minutes. Add the scallions and cook for 1 minute. Stir in the *Korean Soy Ginger Marinade* and cook for 2 minutes. Serve topped with the toasted walnuts.

Serves 4-6 as a side dish

ROLLING LETTUCE CUPS

The first time I had this dish at Betelnut restaurant in San Francisco I thought I had died and gone to heaven. And for all those who are counting carbs, you are going to make this part of your regular repertoire!

1 pound ground turkey (or beef, pork, or a combo)

2 cloves garlic, minced

¼ pound fresh shiitake mushrooms, stems removed, cut into ½-inch dice

2 green onions (white and green parts) cut on the diagonal into ¼-inch wide pieces

½ cup *Korean Soy Ginger Marinade* plus additional for passing

¼ cup coarsely chopped cilantro leaves

1 head butter lettuce, separated into individual leaves

Heat a large skillet or wok over medium-high heat. Add the turkey, stirring to break up the meat and cook until no longer pink, about 5 minutes. Add the garlic and mushrooms and cook until the mushrooms begin to soften, about 3 minutes. Stir in the green onions and the *Korean Soy Ginger Marinade*, and cook for 5 minutes. Add the cilantro, stir well, and remove from the heat.

To serve, divide the turkey filling among the lettuce leaves and drizzle with additional *Marinade*. The lettuce cups can be served already filled or the turkey filling can be placed in the center of a large platter with the lettuce leaves ringing the outer edge for the guests to assemble their own.

Serves 6 as an appetizer or 4 as a light entrée

GINGER-SOY HANGER STEAK

Okay, I am almost embarrassed to put this in the book because it is such a no-brainer, but you just have to try this. I love serving it with steamed baby bok choy or a great salad!

1-1¼ pounds hanger steak (or flank steak)

½ cup *Korean Soy Ginger Marinade*

Place the steak in a ziplock bag. Pour the *Korean Soy Ginger Marinade* over it, zip the bag, and marinate in the refrigerator at least 2 hours or overnight.

Prepare the grill. Grill the steak directly over medium-high heat for approximately 7 minutes per side for medium rare. Remove from the grill, place on a platter, and loosely tent with foil; allow to rest for 10 minutes before slicing against the grain.

Serves 4

Wine Suggestions

Hold the Cabernet and Chardonnay folks! Bust out those wines we really love to drink, but often are afraid to serve. A slightly sweet Riesling or Gewürztraminer will stand up to the bright flavors of this marinade and the sweetness will tame the slight heat from the chiles.
A white Zinfandel will perform admirably as well. If you can't take any sweetness, a smooth Pinot Noir will do just fine.

PAN-ASIAN DIPPING SAUCE & DRESSING

HUNGRY FOR A FRESH-TASTING ASIAN SALAD AND DON'T FEEL LIKE TAKE-OUT OR GOING OUT TO GET IT? PROBLEM SOLVED! CREATE YOUR OWN ASIAN SEAFOOD SALAD WITH OUR *PAN-ASIAN DIPPING SAUCE AND DRESSING.* SO VERSATILE, IT CAN BE USED AS A DIPPING SAUCE FOR ASIAN APPETIZERS OR AS A MARINADE FOR CHICKEN.

ASIAN BROCCOLI SLAW

This salad will take you on a culinary trip to the Far East in about 30 seconds. Serve with grilled meats, and if you want to add another dimension, throw in some grilled pineapple.

One 12-ounce package broccoli slaw (or coleslaw mix)

½ cup *Pan-Asian Dipping Sauce & Dressing*

¼ cup chopped cilantro leaves

¼ cup chopped peanuts

Combine all the ingredients in a bowl, mix well and let sit 30 minutes for flavors to develop before serving.

Serves 4-6 as a side dish

SEARED AHI TUNA SALAD

Your friends and family will be saying "awesome" from the very first bite. So delicious and so healthy, you will be asked to make this again and again.

One 12-ounce package soba noodles

½ English cucumber, cut into matchsticks

½ cup julienned carrots (prepackaged shredded works well)

2 green onions, (white and green parts) sliced on the diagonal into ¼-inch pieces

⅔ cup *Pan-Asian Dipping Sauce & Dressing*

Four 4-ounce sushi grade ahi tuna steaks (about ¾-inch thick)

5 tablespoons sesame seeds

Salt (preferably kosher or sea salt) and freshly ground pepper

1 tablespoon olive oil

Prepare the noodles according to the package directions and drain. Combine the noodles, cucumber, carrots, and green onions in a large bowl with ½ cup of the *Pan-Asian Dipping Sauce & Dressing* and toss well. Divide among four plates.

Place the sesame seeds on a large plate. Sprinkle both sides of the tuna steaks with salt and pepper, and then coat with sesame seeds. Heat the oil in a large skillet over medium-high heat and add the tuna steaks, cooking for just 1 minute per side for medium rare. To serve, slice the tuna steaks thin and overlap the slices in a spiral around the noodles on each plate. Spoon a little more *Dipping Sauce* over the fish.

Serves 4

ASIAN NOODLES

Cold Asian noodles are definitely increasing in popularity and are a great side dish with fish, chicken, or pork. To make a one-dish entrée, simply add some chicken, shrimp, or tofu.

- 1 pound udon noodles or fettuccine
- 2 cups *Pan-Asian Dipping Sauce & Dressing*
- 2 cups fresh sugar snap peas
- 1 cup chopped green onions (white and green parts)
- ½ cup chopped cilantro (optional)
- ½ cup chopped peanuts (optional)

Cook the noodles according to package directions and drain. In a large bowl, combine the cooked noodles, *Pan-Asian Dipping Sauce & Dressing*, snap peas, and green onions. Toss, coating the noodles evenly with the *Dressing*. Garnish with the cilantro and peanuts and serve at room temperature or cold.

Serves 4

Wine Suggestions

A cool, crisp and clean Pinot Gris from California or Oregon is the ideal foil for these Asian-inspired dishes as it cuts through the richness and highlights the flavors.

When tuna or shrimp are added to the equation, a Riesling with its balancing acidity and real or implied sweetness carries the day.

SHRIMP & VEGETABLE SUMMER ROLLS

Don't be afraid of the rice paper, it is really easy to work with. You can use tortillas if you can't find the rice paper. While shrimp is traditional, chicken and pork tenderloin are delicious alternatives.

- 8 sheets rice paper (found in Asian markets)
- 24 large cooked shrimp (31-40 per pound), shelled and deveined (or substitute 2 cups cooked chicken)
- ½ medium English cucumber, cut into ⅛-inch matchsticks
- ¼ cup julienned fresh mint leaves
- ¼ cup julienned fresh basil leaves
- 16 chives, plus additional for garnish (optional)
- ½ cup *Pan-Asian Dipping Sauce & Dressing*

To assemble, fill a large baking sheet with sides (jellyroll pan) with water. Place 2 rice paper rounds in the pan and let soak 1 minute. Spread paper towels on the counter and carefully lift each round out of the water and lay on the towel. Arrange 3 shrimp in a row across the bottom third of the soaked rice paper. Spread one-eighth of the cucumber, mint, basil, and 2 chives horizontally on top of the shrimp. Fold the bottom of the rice paper up over the filling and begin rolling up tightly. At the halfway point, fold in the sides and continue rolling. Transfer to a plate, seam side down, and cover with damp paper towels. Continue with the remaining rice paper and filling.

To serve, cut the rolls in half diagonally, garnish with chives, and pass a bowl of *Pan-Asian Dipping Sauce & Dressing*. Serve immediately or cover with plastic wrap and store in the refrigerator for up to 4 hours.

Makes 8 rolls

SHANGHAI TANGERINE SESAME MARINADE

WE JUST LOVE BIG ASIAN FLAVORS! THIS MARINADE IS PERFECT FOR GRILLED FISH, CHICKEN, MEAT, AND VEGETABLES. IT'S ALSO A DELICIOUS DIPPING SAUCE FOR CHICKEN OR PORK SATÉ, POT STICKERS, EGG ROLLS, OR SHRIMP. STIR-FRIES ARE READY IN MINUTES WHEN YOU CAN ADD FABULOUS FLAVOR FROM ONE BOTTLE!

ASIAN APPETIZERS

It's fun to create an entire party menu around Asian appetizers. It's also so easy that you'll be throwing these types of parties on a regular basis!

Assemble any combination of wontons, egg rolls, pot stickers, spring rolls, sushi, and large cooked shrimp on platters (or for something a little different, place appetizers in Chinese take-out cartons on platters) and serve with *Shanghai Tangerine Sesame Marinade*.

SHANGHAI PIZZA

This is sure to become one of your favorite pizzas. Everyone that has tasted it just loves it so I would suggest making a couple extra. They won't go to waste!

> 1 teaspoon olive oil
> ¼ pound shiitake mushrooms, stems removed, sliced thin
> 1 cup shredded cooked chicken
> ½ cup *Shanghai Tangerine Sesame Marinade*
> 2 flour tortillas (gordita size)
> 1 cup shredded Fontina cheese
> 1 green onion (white and green parts) sliced thin on the diagonal
> ½ cup chopped cilantro leaves

Preheat the oven to 450°F. Place a large baking sheet in the oven. Heat the olive oil in a skillet over medium-high heat. Add the mushrooms and sauté until softened, about 5 minutes. Combine the chicken with ¼ cup of the *Shanghai Tangerine Sesame Marinade* and mix well. Place the tortillas on the hot baking sheet. Spoon the remaining ¼ cup *Marinade* in a thin layer on the tortillas, top with the chicken, mushrooms, and cheese.

Bake for 7-9 minutes, until the cheese melts and the tortillas are crisp. Sprinkle the pizzas with the onions and cilantro, cut into wedges, and serve.

Makes 2 personal-size pizzas or appetizers for 4-6

SESAME SWORDFISH SKEWERS WITH DIPPING SAUCE

This appetizer is a conversation starter for sure and will probably be the talk of the party. You can use any firm fish and for fun, use both black and white sesame seeds.

¾ cup *Shanghai Tangerine Sesame Marinade*

1 pound swordfish steak, cut into 1-inch cubes (about 20 cubes)

20 snow peas

¼ cup sesame seeds, toasted

20 cherry tomatoes

Toothpicks (look for interesting ones at Asian markets)

Preheat the oven to 500°F. Line a baking sheet with aluminum foil. Place the swordfish cubes in a bowl with enough *Shanghai Tangerine Sesame Marinade* to lightly coat them when tossed. Transfer the swordfish cubes to the baking sheet in a single layer. Bake until fish is lightly browned, about 5-7 minutes.

Blanch the snow peas in boiling water for 1 minute, drain, and blot dry. Assemble skewers by first spearing a tomato, followed by a snow pea and then a cube of swordfish. Dip the bottom of the swordfish cube in the sesame seeds and place on a platter. Continue until all skewers are assembled. Serve with a bowl of the *Marinade* for dipping.

Makes 20 skewers for appetizers

꘡

SOBA NOODLES WITH CHICKEN & VEGETABLES

I just love going to noodle houses because they are usually very small and you almost feel like you are in someone's kitchen. You can make this at home and enjoy it any time you crave a comforting bowl of noodles.

8 ounces soba noodles or thin dried spaghetti

1 tablespoon peanut oil or canola oil

1 pound boneless, skinless chicken breasts, cut into strips (or use chicken tenders)

1 large red bell pepper, seeds and ribs removed, cut into thin strips

6 ounces shiitake mushrooms, stems removed and discarded, caps sliced

¾ cup *Shanghai Tangerine Sesame Marinade*

2 green onions (white and green parts) cut diagonally into ¼-inch slices

3 tablespoons chopped peanuts (optional)

2 tablespoons minced fresh basil leaves

Cook the noodles according to package directions. Heat the oil in a large skillet over medium-high heat. Add the chicken and a couple of pinches of salt, and cook 3 minutes, stirring occasionally. Add the peppers and mushrooms and cook 3 minutes. Reduce heat to medium, add the *Shanghai Tangerine Sesame Marinade*, green onions, and noodles and cook another minute until noodles are warmed (add a couple tablespoons of water if sauce is too thick). Serve topped with peanuts and basil.

Serves 4

Wine Suggestions

The rich, savory flavors of the marinade will bring out the best in oaky reds from Zin to Cab. The pizza is made for an old-vine Zinfandel from Paso Robles or the Sierra Foothills. Swordfish skewers can work nicely with a smoky Pinot Noir or a toasty Chardonnay. For the soba noodles and Asian appetizers, either a crisp white Austrian Riesling or delicate red Beaujolais will make your palate smile.

WE BLEND THREE TYPES OF ROASTED CHILES WITH CITRUS TO CREATE THIS MARINADE. USE FROM SUNRISE TO SUNSET IN HUEVOS RANCHEROS, ENCHILADAS, AND BURRITOS—IT'S JUST THAT EASY AND DELICIOUS!

CHICKEN ENCHILADAS

1 cup *Yucatan Three Chiles & Citrus Marinade*

1 tablespoon sugar

¾ pound shredded cooked chicken

1 cup roasted red bell pepper strips

½ medium onion, diced

Eight 6-inch corn tortillas

1½ cups shredded Monterey Jack cheese

Preheat the oven to 375°F. Coat an 11 x 7-inch baking pan with cooking spray and set aside.

In a small bowl stir together the *Yucatan Three Chiles & Citrus Marinade* and sugar. In a medium bowl combine the chicken, roasted peppers, onion and ½ cup of the *Marinade*.

Spoon ¼ cup *Marinade* in the bottom of the baking pan. Divide the chicken mixture among the tortillas and top each with 2 tablespoons of cheese. Roll up tightly and place in the pan, side-by-side. Pour the remaining ¼ cup *Marinade* over the tortillas, cover with foil, and bake for 20 minutes. Top with the remaining cheese and bake for 5 minutes, uncovered.

Serves 4

CHICKEN TORTILLA SOUP

The Yucatan Marinade *gives this soup its body and great flavor—all that just by opening a jar. To make it extra special, top it off with a little sour cream, shredded Jack, cheddar cheese, or all three!*

2 corn tortillas

4 cups chicken stock

3 tablespoons *Yucatan Three Chiles & Citrus Marinade*

3 limes

2 cups shredded cooked chicken

2 Roma tomatoes, seeded and diced

1 avocado, diced

2 green onions (white and green parts) sliced thin on the diagonal

¼ cup chopped cilantro leaves

Preheat the oven to 450°F. Brush both sides of the tortillas with oil, cut each in half, stack the halves together, and cut into ¼-inch strips. Place strips on a baking sheet and bake until crisp, about 10 minutes. Remove from oven and set aside.

Heat the stock in a saucepan and bring to a simmer, add the *Yucatan Three Chiles & Citrus Marinade* and juice of 2 limes. Divide the chicken, tomatoes, avocado, onions, and cilantro among four bowls. Ladle the stock over the ingredients in each bowl and top with equal portions of tortilla strips. Serve with additional lime wedges.

Serves 4

YUCATAN PULLED-PORK SANDWICHES

We served this sandwich using mini buns from Alexis Baking Company at the Napa Valley Wine Auction and people were lined up and coming back again and again! With all the best restaurants in the valley participating, that says a lot.

    1 pork shoulder or pork butt, about 3 pounds

    2 cups *Yucatan Three Chiles & Citrus Marinade*

    Salt (preferably kosher or sea salt) and freshly ground pepper

    Juice of 1 lime

    1 cup Mexican crema or sour cream

    4 hamburger-style buns

    ¼ cup chopped cilantro leaves

Place the pork in a 6-quart slow cooker and pour all but ½ cup of the *Yucatan Three Chiles & Citrus Marinade* over the meat. Set the temperature to medium and cook for 10 hours. (Alternatively you can sear the meat on all sides on the stovetop, cover and then cook in a 350°F oven for about 3½ hours.)

After the meat has cooled down and easily pulls off the bone, pour off the fat and pull the meat off the bone. Discard the bone and shred the meat. Put the shredded meat back in the slow cooker, season with salt and pepper, stir in the remaining ½ cup *Marinade* and cook for another 30 minutes. Mix together the lime juice and Mexican crema. Serve the pulled pork on buns with a drizzle of the lime cream sauce and a sprinkle of cilantro.

Serves 4

Wine Suggestions

The southwest flavor zip of this marinade needs an aromatic white such as Gewürztraminer, Muscat, or Viognier to hold its own; one that is dry or off-dry will pair superbly.

With meats and poultry dishes, a refreshing, young red—Gamay, Grenache, or Pinot Noir—can add dimension and complexity. Any type of sparkling wine, will be superb too.

CHILE & CITRUS CRAB COCKTAIL

Next time you go on a picnic and want to do something fun and different, make this crab cocktail and put it in your cooler. Serve in plastic wine glasses for a surefire crowd pleaser.

    1 green onion (white and green parts) sliced thin on the diagonal

    ½ red bell pepper, seeded and finely diced

    16 cherry tomatoes, halved

    2 tablespoons minced cilantro leaves

    8 ounces fresh crabmeat (picked through to remove shells)

    Juice of 1 lime, plus an additional lime cut into wedges for garnish

    6 tablespoons *Yucatan Three Chiles & Citrus Marinade*

    Tortilla chips

In a medium bowl, combine all of the ingredients except the tortilla chips and lime wedges; mix well. To serve, spoon the crab cocktail into the glass of your choice and tuck in a few tortilla chips and a lime wedge. Pass additional chips for scooping.

Serves 4 as an appetizer

Poultry

Our friend Roxanna's
chickens happily feast on
grapes and garden surplus
at Stonetree Farm

❧

CHAPTER 5

Every Day Classics

CLASSIC BARBECUE SAUCE WITH BALSAMIC

Grilled Cheese Sandwiches

Oven-Braised Baby Back Ribs

Meat Loaf with Barbecue Sauce

Barbecued Corn on the Cob

❋

BARBECUE SAUCE WITH MAPLE & HORSERADISH

Shrimp Cocktail

Maple-Horseradish Barbecued Salmon

Barbecued Oysters

Pizza with Barbecued Chicken

❋

CLASSIC STEAK SAUCE WITH PEACHES

Sour Cream Sauce

Gorgonzola-Stuffed Burgers

Glazed Pork Tenderloin

Grilled Sirloin & Peach Skewers

JANE!

CLASSIC BARBECUE SAUCE WITH BALSAMIC

THE SWEETNESS AND THE ACIDITY OF AGED BALSAMIC VINEGAR FROM ITALY IS WHAT MAKES THIS CONDIMENT SO FABULOUS. NOT JUST FOR GRILLING, THIS SAUCE MAKES A MEAN SLOPPY JOE, TASTES GREAT ON CHICKEN AND BURGERS, AND ADDS DELICIOUS FLAVOR TO BAKED BEANS.

❊

GRILLED CHEESE SANDWICHES

2 tablespoons butter, room temperature

4 slices sourdough bread

4 ounces fresh buffalo mozzarella or smoked cheddar, sliced as thin as possible

2 tablespoons *Classic Barbecue Sauce with Balsamic*

4 small pieces romaine lettuce

Use 1 tablespoon butter to spread one side of the bread slices with. In a large sauté pan melt 1 tablespoon of the butter over medium heat. Place two pieces of bread butter side down in the pan. Add the cheese and top with the other pieces of bread, buttered side up. When the bottom sides are golden brown flip them over, lower the heat, and cook the other side. Remove from the heat when the cheese has melted.

Meanwhile, microwave the *Classic Barbecue Sauce with Balsamic* for about 25 seconds to take the chill off. Open each sandwich, spread with a tablespoon of the *Barbecue Sauce*, top with romaine, and put the sandwich back together.

Serves 2

66

OVEN-BRAISED BABY BACK RIBS

With the sweetness of the balsamic in the barbecue sauce, you will surely enjoy these ribs. You don't have to save these for summertime; they are great all year round and if you add corn bread and Barbecued Corn on the Cob (page 67) you've got a finger-licking feast.

2 racks baby back pork ribs

Salt (preferably kosher or sea salt) and freshly ground pepper

1 cup dry red wine

1 cup *Classic Barbecue Sauce with Balsamic*

Preheat the oven to 325ºF. Season the ribs with salt and pepper to taste and place in a baking dish just large enough to hold them. Pour the wine over the ribs and cover the baking dish with foil. Bake for 2 hours. Uncover, baste the ribs with the wine and brush with *Classic Barbecue Sauce with Balsamic*. Bake for 30 minutes more, uncovered. Remove from oven, brush once again with *Barbecue Sauce*, cut into 2-rib portions and serve immediately.

Serves 4-6

MEAT LOAF WITH BARBECUE SAUCE

Here is a very tasty everyday dish that we just jazzed up with our Barbecue Sauce. If you want a little extra flavor, add some shredded cheese on top during the last 10 minutes in the oven.

> 2 pounds ground beef or ground turkey
>
> 1⅓ cups *Classic Barbecue Sauce with Balsamic*
>
> 1 cup Italian seasoned bread crumbs
>
> 1 small onion, finely diced
>
> 2 eggs, lightly beaten
>
> Salt (preferably kosher or sea salt) and freshly ground pepper

Preheat the oven to 375°F. In a large bowl combine the ground beef, ⅔ cup of the *Classic Barbecue Sauce with Balsamic*, bread crumbs, onion, eggs, and salt and pepper. Form the mixture into a loaf shape on a heavy baking sheet with a lip. Pour the remaining ⅔ cup of *Barbecue Sauce* over the meat loaf, and cover with foil.

Bake for 1 hour. Remove foil and bake for another 10 minutes. Let the meat loaf rest for 10 minutes before slicing and serving.

Serves 4-6

Wine Suggestions

Tomato and balsamic are wine-friendly flavors and this sauce makes it so easy to pair wine!

Grilled cheese sandwiches get a lift when you sip a dry Chenin Blanc. BBQ corn is always good with Chardonnay—use an oaky Chard to pair with the sweet smoke and balsamic. Ribs and meat loaf are classics and nothing's better than a California Zinfandel to match the meat.

BARBECUED CORN ON THE COB

Until I tried this, I would have never put barbecue sauce and corn together but guess what, I did it and loved it. Your kids will too!

> 4 ears fresh corn, husked
>
> Olive oil for brushing
>
> Salt (preferably kosher or sea salt) and freshly ground pepper
>
> 4-6 tablespoons *Classic Barbecue Sauce with Balsamic*

Prepare the grill. Brush the corn with olive oil and sprinkle with salt and pepper. Grill the corn over a low fire for 8 to 10 minutes, turning to cook all sides, until tender and lightly charred. Brush the corn on all sides with *Classic Barbecue Sauce with Balsamic* and grill another minute or two. Transfer to a platter for serving.

Serves 4

BARBECUE SAUCE WITH MAPLE & HORSERADISH

THE CONTRAST OF THE SWEET MAPLE SYRUP WITH THE KICK OF THE HORSERADISH MAKES THIS A TERRIFIC SAUCE TO SLATHER ON ANYTHING YOU PUT ON THE BARBECUE! THE SAUCE CAN ALSO BE POURED OVER A ROAST, CHICKEN, OR A TURKEY BREAST IN YOUR CROCK POT FOR SLOW-COOKED GOODNESS.

SHRIMP COCKTAIL

16 large shrimp (21-24 count)

1 cup *Barbecue Sauce with Maple & Horseradish*

Cook the shrimp in boiling salted water, stirring occasionally, until just cooked through, about 3 minutes. Drain, cool, and shell the shrimp, leaving tails attached. Chill until cold, at least 15 minutes.

To serve, spoon about ¼ cup of the *Barbecue Sauce with Maple & Horseradish* into the middle of 4 martini or margarita glasses and circle with 4 shrimp per glass.

Serves 4 as an appetizer

MAPLE-HORSERADISH BARBECUED SALMON

My friends Sheila and Gary told me that they eat this dish at least once a week. I tried it and can see why. It really doesn't get much easier than this. Leftover salmon is delicious made into a salad for lunch the next day (see Salmon Salad on Butter Lettuce, page 134.)

1 pound salmon fillets, skin and any bones removed, cut into 4 pieces

Salt (preferably kosher or sea salt) and freshly ground pepper

½ cup *Barbecue Sauce with Maple & Horseradish*

Preheat the oven to 450°F. Season the salmon with salt and pepper on both sides. Spoon ¼ cup of the *Barbecue Sauce with Maple & Horseradish* in the bottom of a baking dish large enough to accommodate the fish in a single layer. Pour the remaining ¼ cup of the *Barbecue Sauce* over the fillets. Bake for 10-12 minutes until cooked through, depending on the thickness of the salmon. Serve immediately.

Note: This recipe can also be prepared on a cedar plank on the grill. Soak cedar plank in salted water for 2 hours, then drain. Set grill for indirect grilling and heat to medium-high. Lay the seasoned salmon on the cedar plank and carefully spread the *Barbecue Sauce* over the top and sides. Place the cedar plank on the grate, away from the heat. Cover and grill until cooked through, around 20 to 30 minutes. Transfer the salmon and plank to a platter and serve right off the plank.

Serves 4

BARBECUED OYSTERS

Hog Island Oyster company in nearby Tomales Bay has a barbecued oyster following. We think that we could create our own following with this version, but then we are a little biased.

> 16 large oysters (tell your fishmonger they are for barbecuing)
> ¼-⅓ cup *Barbecue Sauce with Maple & Horseradish*

Prepare the grill. Have an oven mitt and an oyster knife next to the grill and a small bowl for draining off the juices. Place the oysters on the grill over high heat with the cup side down and flat side up. When you see the liquid bubbling around the edges after about 5 minutes, remove the oysters and carefully pour the liquid into the small bowl.

Slip your oyster knife into the back end (small end) of the oyster and pry open shell, toss the top shell. Spoon some *Barbecue Sauce with Maple & Horseradish* on top of each oyster and place the oysters back on the grill. The oysters are ready to serve when the *Barbecue Sauce* begins to bubble. Serve with grilled bread.

Serves 4 as an appetizer

❋

PIZZA WITH BARBECUED CHICKEN

This is probably one of the best pizza's I have ever eaten. I like to make two at a time so that I can take some extra to work the next day. It's also one of those great meals to whip together in no time when you have leftover chicken.

> 1 cup shredded cooked chicken
> ½ cup *Barbecue Sauce with Maple & Horseradish*
> One 16-ounce prebaked thin pizza crust
> ¼ cup thinly sliced red onion rings
> 1 cup shredded smoked Gouda cheese
> ½ cup chopped cilantro leaves

Preheat the oven to 450°F. Combine the chicken with ¼ cup of the *Barbecue Sauce with Maple & Horseradish* and mix well. Spoon the remaining *Barbecue Sauce* in a thin layer on the pizza crust, top with the chicken, onions, and cheese. Bake for 12-15 minutes, until the cheese melts and the crust is crispy. Makes one 12-inch Pizza

Wine Suggestions

Napa Valley offers the ideal wine selections to pair with this Barbecue Sauce. A rich, oak-influenced Chardonnay or Sauvignon Blanc will underscore the maple notes in these seafood and poultry dishes.

If you venture out and try this sauce on meat, a Petite Sirah, Syrah or Zinfandel will be absolutely divine.

THE ADDITION OF THE PEACHES MAKES THIS SAUCE TRULY GOURMET! OF COURSE, WE RECOMMEND YOU USE IT ON YOUR STEAK, RIGHT OFF THE GRILL BUT IT'S ALSO YUMMY ON GRILLED CHICKEN AND FISH AS WELL OR MIX IT WITH A LITTLE MAYO TO JAZZ UP A TURKEY SANDWICH!

SOUR CREAM SAUCE

8 ounces sour cream

1/4 cup *Classic Steak Sauce with Peaches*

Combine ingredients in a medium bowl and mix well. Delicious spooned on baked potatoes, oven-roasted fries, and as a dipping sauce for shrimp or your favorite thick-cut potato or vegetable chips. Leftover sauce will keep for four days in the refrigerator.

Makes 1¼ cups

GORGONZOLA-STUFFED BURGERS

I love burgers and this one is pretty much over the top! Julia taught me that stuffing the cheese inside the meat makes for a creamy, delicious surprise!

> 1½ pounds ground round
> ¼ medium yellow onion, cut into ¼-inch dice
> Salt (preferably kosher or sea salt) and freshly ground pepper
> 2 ounces Gorgonzola or your favorite blue cheese, cut into four cubes
> ½ cup *Classic Steak Sauce with Peaches*
> 8-12 large basil leaves
> 4 large hamburger-style buns

Prepare the grill. In a large bowl, combine the ground beef, onion, a couple pinches of salt and pepper, and work the mixture together with your hands. Divide the mixture into 4 balls. Push a cube of cheese into the center of each ball and squeeze the meat up around it to cover the cheese and flatten into a patty shape about 1-inch thick. (It is important that the beef completely surround the cheese so that it does not leak out when cooking.)

Place the burgers on the grill and cook 3-5 minutes per side depending on how you like your meat cooked. Brush the burgers with the *Classic Steak Sauce with Peaches*, turn, and grill another minute. Repeat with the other side. Grill the buns, cut sides down. To serve, place 2-3 basil leaves on the bottom half of each bun, top with a burger, a spoonful of the *Steak Sauce*, and the top of the bun. Serve with Mediterranean Potato Salad (see page 138.)

Serves 4

GLAZED PORK TENDERLOIN

I always say "think outside of the box", and that holds true here. Even though our Steak Sauce with Peaches *is delicious on steaks, the peaches in the sauce come through nicely with the pork and even on chicken and meatloaf too.*

> Two 12-14 ounce pork tenderloins
>
> Salt (preferably kosher or sea salt) and freshly ground pepper
>
> ½ cup *Classic Steak Sauce with Peaches*

Prepare the grill. Season the pork with salt and pepper and grill over a hot fire for about 5 minutes, turning a few times to develop a nice seared crust. Turn grill to low (or if using charcoal, move to the side away from the direct heat) and grill for 10 minutes more, turning occasionally. Brush the pork with *Classic Steak Sauce with Peaches* and grill for another minute, turn, brush, and grill for another minute until the pork is glazed with *Steak Sauce* on all sides. The pork should be light pink in the center. Transfer to a cutting board, cover with foil, and let rest for 5 minutes before slicing across the grain.

Serves 4-6

Wine Suggestions

Lots of savory flavor here, punched up with Merlot and peaches so make sure the red wines are ready to go!

Are you a Merlot lover? Then pair Gorgonzola-stuffed burgers or the glazed pork tenderloin with a ripe, cherry-flavored Merlot. Red wine heaven! The sirloin and peach skewers are made for a rich, powerful Cabernet Sauvignon.

GRILLED SIRLOIN & PEACH SKEWERS

This is just as pretty as it is fabulous. You can make up the skewers ahead of time and take to a summer evening outdoor concert for a gourmet delight that is easy to eat!

> 2 pounds sirloin tips, cut into 1-inch cubes (or thin strips)
>
> 1 large red onion, cut into wedges
>
> 2 red bell peppers, seeded and cut into 1½-inch squares
>
> 2 peaches, peeled and cut into 8 wedges per peach (or thawed frozen peaches)
>
> ½ cup *Classic Steak Sauce with Peaches* plus additional for serving
>
> 12 wooden skewers soaked in water for 30 minutes
>
> Salt (preferably kosher or sea salt) and freshly ground pepper

Prepare the grill. In a large bowl, combine the meat, onion, pepper, peaches, and *Classic Steak Sauce with Peaches*; mix well. Thread skewers, alternating the sirloin cubes (if using strips, thread on skewers in a zig zag), peaches, peppers, and onions. Season with salt and pepper.

Lightly brush oil on the grill grate. Grill the skewers for 5-7 minutes per side, depending on how you like your meat cooked. Transfer the skewers to a platter and pass a bowl with extra *Steak Sauce*. Serve with crusty bread and rice.

Serves 4

Eggs

Freshly laid eggs
patiently waiting to be turned
into a gourmet treat.
Oh the possibilities—French toast
or scrambled with goat cheese;
mini fritattas or
chocolate souffle—
heavenly!

CHAPTER 6

Classic Herb Rubs

BEEF & BURGER HERB RUB

Oven-Roasted Herbed Salmon Steaks

Outrageous Prime Rib

Rubbed & Roasted Party Nuts

Breakfast Turkey Sausage

PORK & LAMB HERB RUB

Grilled or Roasted Seasonal Vegetables

Napa Valley Shepherd's Pie

Stuffed Pork Tenderloin with Spinach & Feta

Split Pea Soup

FISH & SHELLFISH HERB RUB

Pan-Seared Scallops with Citrus

California Shrimp Boil

Napa Valley Crab Cakes

Trio of Egg-Salad Appetizers

POULTRY HERB RUB

Prosciutto-Wrapped Herbed Chicken Breasts

Spiced Sweet Potato Wedges

Cobb Salad—Napa Valley Style

Grilled Cornish Game Hens

Beef & Burger Herb Rub

A dry rub is a combination of herbs and spices—all you have to do is pour some into a ziplock bag, add your chicken or meat, zip, and shake until coated. Or pour rub onto a plate and roll the meat around before cooking. Add to soups, potato and pasta salads, sandwiches, omelets, or even French fries.

Oven-Roasted Herbed Salmon Fillets

Vegetable oil

Four 4-5 ounce salmon fillets

4 teaspoons *Beef & Burger Herb Rub*

Preheat the oven to 500°F. Oil a large baking sheet with a little vegetable oil. Sprinkle the cut side of the salmon fillets with the *Beef & Burger Herb Rub*. Place the salmon skin side down on the baking sheet. Bake for 12 minutes. Remove from oven, remove skin and serve immediately.

Serves 4

Outrageous Prime Rib

I served this on Christmas Eve and people are still talking about it. Don't wait until then, serve it just because! It's delicious with broccoli rabe, and cauliflower or potato puree.

One 7-8 pound prime rib (3-4 ribs)

Beef & Burger Herb Rub

One 750 ml bottle red wine or 3 cups beef stock

Preheat the oven to 450°F. Sprinkle the meat liberally on both sides with the *Beef & Burger Herb Rub*. Place in a roasting pan, cover loosely with plastic wrap, and let stand at room temperature for up to 1 hour. Remove plastic and place the pan in the center of the oven and roast for 15 minutes. Reduce the heat to 350°F and continue to cook for about 1 hour and 30 minutes until the internal temperature reaches 125°F. Transfer the prime rib to a warm platter and loosely cover with foil. Let rest for 25 minutes before slicing.

While the meat is resting, set the roasting pan on the stovetop. Skim off any fat, add the wine, and bring to a boil over medium-high heat for about a minute, scraping up the bits from the bottom of the pan. Reduce heat and simmer for about 10 minutes. Serve the reduced pan juices with the prime rib.

Serves 6

RUBBED & ROASTED PARTY NUTS

These are delicious and will make your house smell great! I like them served warm just like they do in first class on an airplane. They are healthy too! Try using different rubs for different flavored nuts.

> 1 large egg white
>
> 2 tablespoons *Beef & Burger Herb Rub*
>
> 1 teaspoon salt (preferably kosher or sea salt)
>
> 3 cups roasted almonds or nuts of choice
>
> Olive oil spray
>
> 1 teaspoon sugar (optional)

Preheat the oven to 350°F. In a medium bowl, whisk the egg white until frothy and whisk in the *Beef & Burger Herb Rub* and salt. Add the nuts and stir to coat well. Spray a large baking sheet with olive oil and spread the nuts on the sheet in a single layer. Bake 10-12 minutes. If adding sugar, sprinkle over nuts before baking.

Serve warm or at room temperature. (The nuts can be stored in the freezer and brought to room temp or microwaved for 30 seconds before serving.)

Makes 3 cups

❈

BREAKFAST TURKEY SAUSAGE

I love breakfast sausage, but I know it's not very good for me. So I came up with this easy recipe. Boy, it sure tastes like Jimmy Dean's without the fat!

> 1 pound ground turkey
>
> 4-6 tablespoons *Beef & Burger Herb Rub*

Form the ground turkey into small, sausage-sized patties, about ½-inch thick. Liberally sprinkle both sides of the patties with the *Beef & Burger Herb Rub*. Cook patties in a large, heavy skillet over medium-high heat, for approximately 4 minutes per side, or until they are no longer pink inside. Serve immediately with Moroccan French Toast (page 92).

Serves 4-6

Wine Suggestions

This versatile rub will bring life to a Pinot Noir and pair prefectly with all the recipes, but especially with the salmon steaks.

The prime rib demands what Napa Valley does best...a big red wine! It can be a Cabernet Sauvignon, Merlot, Syrah, or Zinfandel or any other hearty red your heart and palate desire.

FISH & SHELLFISH HERB RUB

Loaded with dill, citrus, herbs, and sea salt, this rub is jam-packed with flavor designed to complement seafood. Sprinkle it on your favorite fish or seafood before grilling, roasting, or pan-searing. Delicious in salad dressings, pasta, eggs, and potatoes.

✖

PAN-SEARED SCALLOPS WITH CITRUS

16 sea scallops or day boat scallops

2 tablespoons *Fish & Shellfish Herb Rub*

1 tablespoon olive oil

Juice of 1 orange

1 tablespoon butter

Sprinkle both sides of the scallops with the *Fish & Shellfish Herb Rub*. Heat the oil in a large skillet over medium-high heat, Add the scallops and sauté until they start to brown, about 2-3 minutes per side. Transfer to a plate and keep warm.

Add the orange juice to the pan, cook over medium heat, stirring to scrape the brown bits from the bottom of the pan, about 1 minute. Add the butter and stir until just melted. Serve 4 scallops per plate with a drizzle of the sauce.

Serves 4 as a starter course

CALIFORNIA SHRIMP BOIL

Imagine a warm summer evening sitting on a sandy beach, happily shelling shrimp and nibbling on corn on the cob and new potatoes. You can make this any time of year. Be sure to enjoy it with crusty bread and wine.

½ cup *Fish & Shellfish Herb Rub*

1 tablespoon kosher salt

One 750 ml bottle dry white wine

2 pounds medium red potatoes, quartered

4 ears sweet corn, husked and cut into 3 pieces

2 pounds uncooked medium shrimp in the shell (31-40 count)

4 sausages (spicy chicken or turkey precooked sausages), sliced on the diagonal into 6 pieces

Fill an 8-quart stockpot half full with water, cover, and bring to a boil. Add the *Fish & Shellfish Herb Rub*, salt, wine, potatoes, and corn. Cover and cook for 7 minutes. Add the shrimp and sausages and cook for another 3 minutes.

Remove 1 cup of the cooking liquid and set aside. Remove the pot from the heat and pour the shrimp boil ingredients into a large colander to drain. Pile the shrimp boil onto a large platter and pour some of the reserved cooking liquid on top.

Serve with bowls of our *Barbecue Sauce* or cocktail sauce for dipping shrimp, *Mustard* for dipping sausages, and butter for slathering on the corn.

Serves 4

Napa Valley Crab Cakes

I have several friends who are crab-cake aficionados and these have passed the test! I know this goes without saying, but just in case, be sure to use real crab!

- 1 tablespoon plus ½ teaspoon *Fish & Shellfish Herb Rub*
- 1 cup fresh bread crumbs (made from 2 pieces day old bread, pulsed in a blender)
- 2 large eggs, beaten
- 1 tablespoon Dijon mustard
- 1 pound fresh lump crabmeat
- 2 green onions (white and green parts) cut into ¼-inch rings
- ½ cup yogurt
- Juice of 1 lemon
- 1 teaspoon olive oil

Mix together 1 tablespoon of the *Fish & Shellfish Herb Rub* and the bread crumbs and set aside. In a large bowl, stir together the eggs and mustard; add the crabmeat, onions, and bread crumbs and mix gently to combine. Form the crab mixture into 8 patties. (You can make these up to 1 day ahead, cover, and refrigerate. Bring to room temperature before proceeding.)

Prepare the sauce by combining the remaining ½ teaspoon of *Herb Rub*, the yogurt, and the lemon juice.

In a nonstick skillet heat the olive oil over medium heat. Add enough cakes to the pan without crowding and cook about 3 minutes per side until they start to turn a golden brown. Remove from skillet and keep warm while cooking the remaining cakes. Serve 2 crab cakes with a dollop of yogurt sauce per plate as a first course. Lightly dressed arugula is a nice addition to the plate for a light lunch.

Serves 4

Wine Suggestions

Flavorings here are white-wine friendly; citrus, dill, tarragon, and sea salt add zest to a Sauvignon Blanc, Pinot Gris, or Viognier.

The scallops with orange in the sauce just scream for Viognier! Shrimp is perfect with Sauvignon but go for Chardonnay if you like richer flavors. Crab cakes are also best with Chardonnay but try a dry (brut) Sparkling wine with the egg-salad appetizers.

⁜

Trio of Egg-Salad Appetizers

This is taking egg salad to a whole new level. And if you have any of the egg mixture left, make an egg salad sandwich the next day. Personally I would wrap it in a whole wheat tortilla!

- 4 large hard-boiled eggs, finely chopped
- 2 tablespoons finely diced celery
- ¼ cup mayonnaise
- 2 teaspoons *Fish & Shellfish Herb Rub*
- ½ avocado, chopped
- Juice of ½ lemon
- 1 head Belgian endive, rinsed and leaves pulled apart
- 1 English cucumber, peeled and sliced into thin rounds
- 4 small tomatoes (about 1½ inch diameter), halved and seeded
- Salt (preferably kosher or sea salt) and freshly ground pepper

Combine the eggs, celery, mayonnaise, and *Fish & Shellfish Herb Rub* in a medium bowl. In a small bowl, mash together the avocado and lemon juice. Stir into the egg mixture and season with salt and pepper. Spoon the egg salad into the tomato halves and endive leaves and onto the cucumber rounds. Place the appetizers creatively on a platter and serve.

Serves 4-6 as appetizers

WE HAVE CREATED OUR RUBS AND NAMED
THEM WITH A PARTICULAR INGREDIENT IN MIND,
BUT DON'T FEEL LIMITED BY THAT. IN THIS CASE
THE *PORK & LAMB HERB RUB* IS EQUALLY DE-
LICIOUS ON CHICKEN, FISH, OR VEGETABLES
AND IN EGGS, PASTAS, SOUPS, OR SALADS.

GRILLED OR ROASTED SEASONAL VEGETABLES

One of my favorite uses of herb rubs is on
grilled or roasted vegetables. Try using different rubs for variety. Experiment to find your
favorites.

Cut up a variety of seasonal vegetables—zucchini, eggplant, and bell peppers in the summer, and winter squash, parsnips, carrots,
and potatoes in the winter.

Toss the vegetables with olive oil, sprinkle
generously with *Pork & Lamb Herb Rub* and
either grill or roast in the oven at 450°F until
cooked through and caramelized in spots on
the outside.

NAPA VALLEY SHEPHERD'S PIE

I was cooking for some friends on a rainy winter night (we have a lot of those in the Napa Valley) who were low-carbing it. I wanted something hearty and I love shepherd's pie so I swapped out the potatoes with the cauliflower and it was a hit!

3 tablepoons olive oil

1 head cauliflower, cut into small pieces

¼ cup low-fat milk

Salt (preferably kosher or sea salt)

¾ pound fresh baby spinach or 9 ounces frozen, thawed and squeezed dry

1 pound ground pork, lamb, turkey, beef, or any combination

1 tablespoon *Pork & Lamb Herb Rub*

1 large egg, beaten

¼ cup grated Parmesan or Asiago cheese

Preheat the oven to 400°F. Coat a 9 x 13-inch baking dish with 1 tablespoon of the olive oil and set aside. Prepare a steamer basket, add the cauliflower, and cook until very soft, about 10 minutes. Transfer to a large bowl, add the milk and a couple of pinches of salt. Mash with a potato masher. Set aside.

Heat 1 tablespoon of the olive oil in a large skillet over medium-high heat. Add the spinach, stirring con-stantly until it is wilted and soft, remove from heat and set aside in a bowl. In the same skillet, set over high heat, add the ground meat. As it starts to brown, stir in the *Pork & Lamb Herb Rub*, and a couple of pinches of salt, and mix well. Reduce heat to medium and cook until the meat is completely cooked through.

To assemble, spread the cooked meat evenly in the bottom of the prepared baking dish, add the spinach, and top with the cauliflower. Pour the egg evenly over the entire dish. Sprinkle with the cheese and cover with foil. Bake for about 20 minutes. Remove foil and bake until the mixture is slightly browned and heated all the way through, about 10-15 minutes more. Remove from oven and let stand for 5 minutes before serv-ing. Drizzle with the last tablespoon of olive oil, cut, and serve.

Serves 6

STUFFED PORK TENDERLOIN WITH SPINACH & FETA

This recipe takes pork tenderloin to a new level. It has some of my favorite flavors, and if you have any roasted red bells hanging around, put those in too!

- 2 tablespoons olive oil
- ½ cup minced yellow onion
- 2 packages frozen spinach, thawed and squeezed dry
- Two 1-pound pork tenderloins
- 5 ounces feta cheese, crumbled
- 5 tablespoons *Pork & Lamb Herb Rub*
- 1 cup dry white wine
- 1 cup low-salt chicken broth
- Kitchen string
- Salt (preferably kosher or sea salt) and freshly ground pepper

Preheat the oven to 350°F. Heat 1 tablespoon of the olive oil in a large skillet over medium-high heat. Add the onions and sauté until they begin to soften, about 5 minutes. Add the spinach and sauté for a couple of minutes until the moisture evaporates. Remove from heat and let cool.

Cut through each pork tenderloin lengthwise to within ½-inch of cutting all the way through. Open up the pork like a book and pound out each side until it's about ¼-inch thick. Distribute the spinach over each tenderloin and top with the cheese. Roll each tenderloin jelly-roll style from the long side, and tie with string in 5 places. Coat the outside of each tenderloin with 2½ tablespoons of the *Pork & Lamb Herb Rub*. Let stand 30 minutes.

Heat the remaining olive oil in an ovenproof skillet over medium-high heat. Add tenderloins and sauté, turning to brown all sides, about 7 minutes total. Place the skillet in oven. Roast the pork until a thermometer inserted into thickest part registers 150°F, about 35 minutes. Transfer the tenderloins to a platter; cover loosely with foil. Place the same skillet over medium heat, and add the wine and broth. Boil until the sauce thickens, scraping up browned bits, about 10 minutes. Season with salt and pepper. To serve, remove strings from the pork and cut into ½-inch-thick slices. Spoon the sauce over the pork.

Serves 6

SPLIT PEA SOUP

Pureed vegetable and legume soups are my favorites. Just by drizzling a little extra-virgin olive oil or white truffle oil, this soup is taken to a new level.

- One 16-ounce bag dried split peas
- 2 quarts chicken stock
- 1 medium onion, diced
- 2 carrots, diced
- 1 leftover ham bone with meat left on or 2 smoked ham hocks
- 2 tablespoons *Pork & Lamb Herb Rub*
- White truffle oil or extra-virgin olive oil (optional)
- Crème fraîche or sour cream (optional)

Rinse the peas in cold water, place in a large stockpot with the chicken stock, bring to a boil, and boil for 2 minutes. Remove from heat, cover, and let stand for 1 hour. Add the onions, carrots, ham, and *Pork & Lamb Herb Rub*, bring to a boil. Reduce heat to low and simmer, covered, for approximately 2 - 2½ hours, at which point the peas should be very tender and falling apart.

Remove the ham from the soup, cut the meat from the bones and put the meat back in the soup. Then puree the soup in a blender or food processor. Return the soup to the stockpot, heat thoroughly, and serve with a dollop of crème fraîche and/or a drizzle of white truffle or extra-virgin olive oil if desired.

Serves 8

Wine Suggestions

A savory mix of herbs and spices makes this rub wine-friendly.

Roasted veggies will pair with any wine! Same for the shepherds pie—white or red are perfect, especially a heavier Merlot or Viognier. The pork tenderloin will go very well with a medium-bodied Cabernet or Syrah, while Chardonnay is the wine for split pea soup.

With herb blends on hand you can easily take food to the next level. Add a pinch or a sprinkle to season your chicken dishes, but you can also use it on potato or pasta salads, scrambled eggs or omelets, soups and stews, casseroles, sauces, baked potatoes, scalloped potatoes and more.

PROSCIUTTO-WRAPPED HERBED CHICKEN BREASTS

4 boneless, skinless chicken breast halves

2 ounces soft fresh goat cheese, cut into 4 pieces

4 teaspoons *Poultry Herb Rub*

4 thin slices prosciutto

Preheat the oven to 375°F. Cut a slit into the side of each chicken breast creating a pocket. Fill each pocket with goat cheese. Season the chicken breasts with a sprinkle of *Poultry Herb Rub*. Wrap each chicken breast with a piece of prosciutto, going around the middle enclosing the pocket slit in the side of each breast. Place on a baking sheet.

Bake until the prosciutto starts to brown and the chicken is cooked through, about 25 minutes. Serve with the pan juices spooned over the top.

Serves 4

SPICED SWEET POTATO WEDGES

These wedges are a great alternative to traditional French fries. Delicious yet healthy! For a fun presentation you can serve them like some Napa restaurants do in cones that you make from parchment or brown kraft paper.

3 large sweet potatoes, about 2 pounds, scrubbed but unpeeled

1 tablespoon plus 1 teaspoon olive oil

1 tablespoon plus 1 teaspoon *Poultry Herb Rub*

Salt (preferably kosher or sea salt)

Preheat oven to 400°F. Line a rimmed baking sheet with foil. Cut the potatoes in half lengthwise and cut each half into 1-inch-thick wedges. In a large bowl, combine the potatoes, oil, *Poultry Herb Rub,* and salt to taste. Toss to coat evenly.

Arrange the potatoes on a baking sheet in a single layer. Bake until the wedges are golden on the bottom, about 15 minutes. Using a spatula, turn the potatoes and bake until golden all over, about 15 minutes more. Serve warm with Sour Cream Sauce (page 70) for dipping.

Serves 4

Cobb Salad—Napa Valley Style

At the Boone Fly Café in Caneros, they probably do the best job with this classic salad of any restaurant I know. The chicken and the bacon are served warm and the salad is tossed—it totally makes it!

    2 boneless chicken breasts

    2 tablespoons *Poultry Herb Rub*

    12 cups (12 ounces) mixed field greens

    2 hearts of romaine, chopped

    6 green onions (white and green parts) sliced

    4 strips crisp bacon, crumbled

    1 avocado, cubed

    2 tomatoes, cubed

    4 ounces Gorgonzola or blue cheese, crumbled

    Salad dressing of your choice (try our *Merlot with Walnut Oil*)

    Salt (preferably kosher or sea salt)

Prepare the grill or broiler. Cut the chicken breasts in half so you have four pieces all about the same size. Cover the chicken with the *Poultry Herb Rub*. Grill for about 4 minutes per side until cooked through.

In a large salad bowl, combine the mixed greens, romaine, and green onions. Add the bacon, avocado, tomatoes, and cheese.

When the chicken is coming off the grill, toss the salad with your favorite dressing. Then divide the salad mixture among four large dinner plates. Place the chicken breasts on top, add a little salt and serve!

Serves 4

Wine Suggestions

These herb rub recipes will sing in perfect harmony when matched with fuller-bodied whites such as Chardonnay, Viognier, and barrel-fermented Sauvignon Blanc.

All of these wines possess the ideal texture and weight to perfectly complement the richness and flavor imbued by the poultry spices.

Grilled Cornish Game Hens

Cornish game hens have kind of been forgotten, but whenever I serve them, everyone raves. This recipe is super easy and so flavorful. Toss a salad and you have an almost effortless yet fabulous meal!

    4 Cornish game hens, halved (ask your butcher to do this for you)

    2-3 tablespoons *Poultry Herb Rub*

Prepare the grill. Cover the hens with the *Poultry Herb Rub* and place them skin side down on the hot grill. Grill for 10 minutes, turn, and cook another 10 minutes or until a thermometer inserted into the thickest part reads 160°F. Serve immediately with My Favorite Bread Salad (page 28) or a more traditional wild rice pilaf and a green vegetable.

Serves 4

CHAPTER 7

Global Herb Rubs

ASIAN ACCENTS HERB RUB

Seared Tuna "Burger"

Spiced Jasmine Rice

Asian Potato Salad

Chicken-Coconut Milk Soup

MEDITERRANEAN MEDLEY HERB RUB

Mediterranean Roasted Potatoes

Grilled Swordfish with Herb Butter

Room-Temperature Pasta

Macaroni & Cheese with a Twist

MIGUEL'S MEXICAN FIESTA HERB RUB

Fiesta Guacamole

Black Bean & Charred Corn Salad with Avocado

Fabulous Fish Tacos

Breakfast Burrito

MYSTIC MOROCCAN HERB RUB

Spiced Carrots with Citrus

Moroccan French Toast

Lentil Soup with Herbed Yogurt

Spiced Ground Lamb with Yogurt Sauce

NAPA VALLEY MERITAGE HERB RUB

Rubbed & Roasted Tomatoes

Scrambled Eggs with Herbs & Goat Cheese

Grilled Lamb Chops with Herb Rub

Grilled Chicken with Herb Rub

SPICY AMERICAN BARBECUE HERB RUB

Spicy Herb Butter

New York Strip Steaks with Seared Tomato Vinaigrette

Flank Steak with a Mustard Rub

Assorted Mini Burgers

JANE!

ASIAN ACCENTS HERB RUB

When you open the tin, the aromas of this rub will transport you to the Far East. It's so versatile, you'll use it on everything from vegetables to rice, and grilled meats to stir-fries. It is as beautiful as it is delicious, with black and white sesame seeds, dried chiles, and Asian spices making up the mix.

✳

SEARED TUNA "BURGER"

1 tablespoon sesame oil

¼ cup mayonnaise

⅓ cup yogurt

1 tablespoon plus 4 teaspoons *Asian Accents Herb Rub*

Four 4-ounce sushi-grade ahi tuna steaks (about ¾-inch thick)

4 buns (ciabatta style if you can find them)

1 avocado, sliced

Prepare the grill. In a small bowl, mix together the sesame oil, mayonnaise, yogurt, and 1 tablespoon of the *Asian Accents Herb Rub*; set aside. Grill the cut side of the buns and set aside.

Sprinkle each side of the tuna steaks with a half teaspoon of *Herb Rub* (4 teaspoons total) and press rub into the steaks. Grill for about a minute per side for tuna medium rare. To serve, spread tops and bottoms of buns with the mayonnaise spread, place a tuna steak on each bun, and top with avocado.

Serves 4

86

SPICED JASMINE RICE

Simple, yet so good, you'll feel like you've gone to Asia. Serve with stir-fried vegetables or grilled chicken or steak. Or just eat the rice by itself. Delicious!

1½ to 2 cups water, depending on the type of rice you're using

1 cup rice (long grain, jasmine, or basmati)

1 tablespoon *Asian Accents Herb Rub*

Bring the water to a boil in a medium saucepan. Add the rice and the *Asian Accents Herb Rub*. Stir a couple of times, cover, and reduce heat to low. Cook for 15 minutes. Remove from heat and let stand, covered, for 5 –10 minutes before fluffing with a fork. Serve immediately.

Variation: Try any of our herb rubs for a different flavored rice; our global-inspired rubs are perfect accompaniments to your favorite cuisine.

Serves 4 as a side dish

ASIAN POTATO SALAD

Okay, you are probably thinking this is another boring potato salad recipe. But trust me on this one; this potato salad will turn some heads. I had something similar at a Japanese deli at the San Francisco Ferry Plaza and was so inspired!

4 Russet potatoes (about 4 pounds), peeled and cut into bite-size chunks

½ cup mayonnaise (or more if you like it a little creamier like I do)

½ large onion, diced

¼ cup *Asian Accents Herb Rub*

1 head romaine lettuce, chopped (remove flabby outer leaves and discard)

1 cup edamame (shelled soy beans; these are available in the fresh or frozen food section)

Cook the potatoes in salted boiling water until softened but still firm, about 10 minutes. Drain and put the potatoes in a large bowl. Cook the edamame according to the package instructions, drain, and add to the potatoes. Add the onion and lettuce. In a small bowl combine the mayonnaise and *Asian Accents Herb Rub*, add to potatoes, toss it all together, and serve!

Serves 6

❖

CHICKEN-COCONUT MILK SOUP

I used to think you could only get this soup at a Thai restaurant. Lemongrass, coconut milk, and straw mushrooms are available in most grocery stores, and the recipe is so easy you can make it at home.

3 stalks fresh lemongrass

32 ounces chicken stock

Two 13.5-ounce cans unsweetened coconut milk

3 tablespoons *Asian Accents Herb Rub*

4 cooked boneless chicken thighs, skinned and cubed

1 teaspoon cornstarch

One 15-ounce can straw mushrooms, drained

4 green onions (white and green parts), chopped

6 cups (about 6 ounces) baby spinach leaves

2 tablespoons lime juice

¼ cup chopped cilantro leaves

Lime wedges, for serving

Peel the outer layer of the lemongrass and mince the bottom 2 inches, you should have about 1½ tablespoons. In a large stockpot combine 3¾ cups of the chicken stock with the coconut milk and bring to a boil over high heat. Reduce the heat slightly and add the lemongrass, *Asian Accents Herb Rub*, and chicken. Simmer for 10 minutes.

Mix the cornstarch with the remaining ¼ cup chicken stock and add it in a steady stream to the simmering soup, stirring constantly until the soup thickens slightly. Add the mushrooms and let cook another 5 minutes. Add the onions, spinach, lime juice, and cilantro. Cook until heated all the way through. Serve immediately with the lime wedges on the side.

Serves 4-6

Wine Suggestions

The allure of Asian spices brings out the best in aromatic whites, where more subtle whites would be easily overpowered.
Look for Gewürztraminer, Muscat, Riesling, and Viognier to bring tears of joy to your eyes with these recipes. Whether or not you're in a celebratory mood, a sparkling wine or Champagne is a marvel to the senses too.

MEDITERRANEAN MEDLEY HERB RUB

A combination of 11 to 13 herbs, spices, and sea salt make up our rubs, and this one has the flavors of the Mediterranean; oregano, garlic, and rosemary are key players. Think Greek salad, Italian pasta or French fries as a few ideas for using this rub. You can combine it with olive oil to form a paste to rub on meat, poultry, or fish before grilling or roasting.

MEDITERRANEAN ROASTED POTATOES

2 pounds waxy new potatoes (about 2 to 3 inches in diameter), peeled and halved

4 teaspoons olive oil

4 teaspoons *Mediterranean Medley Herb Rub*

Salt (preferably kosher or sea salt)

Preheat the oven to 500°F. Position a rack in the middle of the oven. Place the potatoes in a roasting pan large enough to hold them in a single layer. Drizzle the olive oil over the potatoes. Toss well to coat the potatoes and the bottom of the pan. Sprinkle with the *Mediterranean Medley Herb Rub* and a pinch or two of salt and toss again.

Roast the potatoes for 15 minutes. Turn with a metal spatula and roast another 10-15 minutes until they are golden. Serve immediately for a nice crisp exterior with a fluffy interior.

Serves 4 as a side dish

GRILLED SWORDFISH WITH HERB BUTTER

This dish reminds me of eating in a small café on the coast. I like to serve it with mashed cauliflower drizzled with olive oil and sea salt.

2 tablespoons *Mediterranean Medley Herb Rub*

1 stick (½ cup) unsalted butter, at room temperature

Six 6-ounce swordfish steaks

Salt (preferably kosher or sea salt) and freshly ground pepper

Mix the *Mediterranean Medley Herb Rub* and butter together in a food processor or small bowl. On a sheet of plastic wrap, form the butter into a rectangle about 6 x 2 inches. Roll into a log and twist each end. Freeze for about 45 minutes, until the butter is somewhat solid. (You can store the butter in the refrigerator for about 6 weeks and about 9 weeks in the freezer.)

Prepare the grill. Season the swordfish with salt and pepper. Grill for about 3-5 minutes per side, depending on the thickness of the swordfish steaks. To serve, remove wrap from herb butter and slice into 1-inch coins. When serving outside, place the butter coins in a bowl of ice water until ready to serve. Place a coin on each fish steak as it is removed from grill. Serve with grilled vegetables and Room Temperature Pasta (page 89).

Serves 6

ROOM-TEMPERATURE PASTA

I used to stress out trying to serve a pasta dish hot, but never succeeded in getting everyone to the table in time, so I just decided that it was supposed to be at room temperature—hence the name. And it really is delicious.

12 ounces gemelli pasta or your favorite dried pasta

¼ cup extra-virgin olive oil

1 tablespoon plus 1 teaspoon *Mediterranean Medley Herb Rub*

½ cup grated Parmesan cheese, plus 2 tablespoons for topping

Fill a large pot with water and bring to a boil, adding a generous amount of salt when it boils. Cook the pasta in the salted boiling water according to the package instructions. Drain. While the pasta is draining, heat the oil over medium heat in the pasta pot and stir in the *Mediterranean Medley Herb Rub*. Add the pasta and stir to coat well. Remove from the heat and stir in the ½ cup of the cheese. Sprinkle the remaining 2 tablespoons cheese on top before serving.

Serves 6

Wine Suggestions

One could do no wrong by pairing a Napa Valley Chardonnay with the swordfish or a Napa Sauvignon Blanc with the macaroni and cheese. In general though, the savory herbs of this rub will match expertly with reds such as Napa Valley Cabernet Sauvignon and Merlot, or Mediterrnean-based red varieties such as Grenache (Côtes du Rhône, Chateauneuf du Pape), Tempranillo (Rioja) and Sangiovese (Chianti).

MACARONI & CHEESE WITH A TWIST

I suggested this recipe to a friend and she pooh-poohed me, saying her days of mac and cheese were long gone. I served it to her and she was blown away! I think her memory of mac and cheese was out of a blue box.

8 ounces dried orecchiette

2 tablespoons olive oil

1 small onion, finely diced

1 tablespoon flour

1 tablespoon *Mediterranean Medley Herb Rub*

1 cup low-fat milk

1 tomato, seeded and finely diced

1 cup assorted shredded cheeses (Parmesan, feta, cheddar, Gruyere or goat), reserve ¼ cup for topping

Prepare the pasta according to package instructions. Preheat the oven to 375°F. Coat a 9 x 13-inch baking dish with 1 tablespoon of the olive oil.

Heat the remaining tablespoon of olive oil in a large skillet over medium-high heat. Add the onions and cook until softened and beginning to brown, about 5 minutes. Add the flour, stirring constantly; add the *Mediterranean Medley Herb Rub* and stir until well mixed. Slowly pour in half the milk, continuing to stir as it thickens, finish with the remaining milk. Once thickened, reduce heat to low and add 1 cup of the shredded cheese, continuing to stir. Once completely mixed, add the tomatoes and pasta. Toss until pasta is evenly covered with sauce. Pour into a baking dish and sprinkle with the remaining cheese and a little *Herb Rub*. Bake for about 20-25 minutes or until golden brown.

Serves 4 as a light entrée or 8 as a side dish

MIGUEL'S MEXICAN FIESTA HERB RUB

LIMES, CHILES, CILANTRO, AND CUMIN ARE JUST A FEW OF THE MANY INGREDIENTS THAT MAKE UP THIS RUB. IT'S TERRIFIC RUBBED ON PORK TENDERLOIN, FLANK STEAK, CHICKEN, SHRIMP, OR RED SNAPPER BEFORE GRILLING, SERVED WITH PILES OF CORN TORTILLAS AND A DRIZZLE OF SOUR CREAM.

※

FIESTA GUACAMOLE

2 ripe avocados, chopped

1 tablespoon *Miguel's Mexican Fiesta Herb Rub*

2 Roma tomatoes, seeded and chopped

½ small onion, diced

Juice of 2 limes

Salt (preferably kosher or sea salt) to taste

In a medium bowl combine all the ingredients. Serve with a basket of tortilla chips.

Serves 4

BLACK BEAN & CHARRED CORN SALAD WITH AVOCADO

Lots of the people who work with me are Hispanic and they always laugh at me because I love their food so much. I made this for them and they applauded—muy delicioso!

> 1 tablespoon olive oil
>
> 2 cups corn kernels (from 2 large ears, or frozen)
>
> ½ small red onion, peeled and diced
>
> 1 tablespoon *Miguel's Mexican Fiesta Herb Rub*
>
> One 15-ounce can black beans, rinsed and drained
>
> ½ cup minced basil leaves
>
> 1 cup seeded and diced tomatoes (about 3 medium Roma)
>
> 1 avocado, diced
>
> 3 tablespoons lime juice (1½ limes)
>
> Salt (preferably kosher or sea salt) and freshly ground pepper

Heat the oil in a large skillet over medium-high heat. Add the corn, onion, and *Miguel's Mexican Fiesta Herb Rub*, and sauté 5 to 7 minutes, until corn begins to brown (or char), stirring frequently. Remove from heat and allow to cool.

Add the remaining ingredients to the corn mixture, stir to combine, and season to taste with salt and pepper. For an interesting serving idea, spoon the salad into avocado halves.

Variation: Grill the corn on the cob before cutting kernels off. If serving in avocado halves, brush with oil and sprinkle with *Herb Rub*, grill cut side down until grill marks appear. Spoon salad into grilled avocados.

Serves 4 to 6

FABULOUS FISH TACOS

Not your typical tacos here, these are loaded with fresh ingredients. I bet you are wondering about the mayo—it sounds weird but it makes the taco!

1 pound halibut, sea bass, or cod fillets, bones removed

2-3 tablespoons *Miguel's Mexican Fiesta Herb Rub*

8 small corn or flour tortillas

¼ cup mayonnaise

1 red bell pepper, roasted, ribs and seeds removed, cut into strips

1 avocado, cut into thin slices

½ red onion, thinly sliced

2 jalapeños, seeds and ribs removed, cut into slivers (optional)

¼ cup cilantro leaves

½ cup feta cheese (or queso fresco)

1 lime, quartered

Salt (preferably kosher or sea salt)

Prepare the grill or broiler. Sprinkle the fish with *Miguel's Mexican Fiesta Herb Rub*. Grill or broil fish until opaque and flakey, about 5-8 minutes depending on the thickness of the fish. Wrap the tortillas in a couple of wet paper towels and microwave for 1-2 minutes or until hot and steamy.

To assemble, spread a little mayonnaise on each tortilla and divide the fish, roasted pepper, avocado, onion, jalapeño, and cheese among the tortillas. Sprinkle with cilantro, a squeeze of lime juice, and pinch of salt. Fold the tortillas over and place two on each plate—you are ready for a fiesta!

Serves 4

※

BREAKFAST BURRITO

If you don't eat meat, this is just as good without it. You can serve these for breakfast, lunch, or dinner.

4 eggs

¼ cup milk (low-fat or nonfat is fine)

1 tablespoon butter

⅓ cup diced onion

½ pound ground beef or turkey

1 tablespoon *Miguel's Mexican Fiesta Herb Rub*

½ cup shredded Fontina or crumbled goat cheese

4 flour tortillas

Mayonnaise or sour cream (optional)

½ cup pico de gallo salsa or any chunky-style salsa

In a large bowl beat the eggs with the milk until frothy. Melt the butter in a large sauté pan over medium-high heat. Add the onions and cook until translucent. Add the meat and *Miguel's Mexican Fiesta Herb Rub*. Stir occasionally until meat is cooked. Add the egg mixture and continue to cook, stirring frequently, until eggs just begin to set. Add the cheese and stir until it begins to melt. Remove pan from stove.

Microwave the tortillas for about 30 seconds. Spread with a little mayonnaise. Divide the egg mixture evenly across the center of the 4 tortillas, and top with 2 tablespoons of salsa. Take each side of the tortilla and fold in a couple of inches, then roll into the traditional burrito shape.

Serves 4-6

Wine Suggestions

Classic Central American flavors such as roasted cumin, garlic, and chiles are very similar to the flavors oak barrels impart to wine.

So pair your fish tacos with a barrel-aged Chardonnay, enjoy the black bean salad with a smoky Pinot Gris or Viognier and, if you dare, have a dollop of oaky Zinfandel with your breakfast burrito!

Mystic Moroccan Herb Rub

Food can transport you to another country. The spices of Morocco—dried chiles, lemon peel, and garlic—complement lamb, chicken, couscous, and vegetables. Sprinkle in soups, yogurt for dips, rice and grain dishes, or rub on chicken or lamb for kebabs.

Spiced Carrots with Citrus

1½ pounds carrots, peeled and cut on the diagonal into ¼-inch thick pieces (or use the bagged peeled baby carrots)

2 tablespoons olive oil

2 tablespoons *Mystic Moroccan Herb Rub*

Juice of 1 orange

Bring a large pot of salted water to a boil. Add the carrots, bring back to a boil and cook 2 minutes (if using the baby carrots you may need to cook just a minute longer) until crisp but cooked through. Drain the carrots in a colander.

Place the pot back on the stove over medium heat and add the olive oil and *Mystic Moroccan Herb Rub,* heat for about 1 minute. Add the carrots and orange juice and stir to coat the carrots evenly. Cook for another minute or two until the carrots are heated through.

Serves 4 as a side dish

Moroccan French Toast

I love savory and sweet together so I tried this combination one morning and couldn't believe how good it was. I think you will agree!

6 large eggs
¾ cup milk
1 tablespoon *Mystic Moroccan Herb Rub*
Butter
8 slices day-old sourdough bread or 12 baguette slices
Maple syrup
Confectioners' sugar (optional)

Preheat the oven to 250°F. In a large mixing bowl, whisk together the eggs, milk, and *Mystic Moroccan Herb Rub* until frothy, about 3 minutes. Heat a large skillet over medium-high heat with enough butter to cover the surface. Submerge the bread in the egg mixture, 2-3 pieces at a time. Place the soaked bread in the hot pan. Cook until golden brown, turn, and repeat. Remove the French toast from the pan and place on a baking sheet in the oven. Repeat with the bread and egg mixture, adding more butter to the pan to prevent the bread from sticking. Serve warm with more butter, warm maple syrup, and/or confectioners' sugar and your favorite fruit preserves!

Serves 4

LENTIL SOUP WITH HERBED YOGURT

This is a hearty soup that is just delicious. Feel free to sprinkle a little more Mystic Moroccan Herb Rub as a garnish along with the yogurt if you so desire.

  1½ tablespoons olive oil

  1 medium onion, diced

  2 medium carrots, diced

  2 cloves garlic, minced

  1 tablespoon *Mystic Moroccan Herb Rub*

  1½ cups lentils (preferably French green)

  6 cups (or more) chicken broth or vegetable broth

  1 tablespoon balsamic vinegar

  Salt (preferably kosher or sea salt) and freshly ground pepper

  ½ cup plain yogurt

  ¼ cup minced mint leaves

Heat the oil in a large pot over medium heat. Add the onions, carrots, and garlic and sauté until they begin to soften, about 10 minutes. Add the *Mystic Moroccan Herb Rub* and lentils and stir 2 minutes. Add the broth and bring to a boil. Reduce heat, cover, and simmer until lentils are tender, about 30 minutes, stirring occasionally and adding more broth if the soup is too thick. Stir in the vinegar and season with salt and pepper to taste.

In a small bowl, whisk together the yogurt and mint. Season with salt and pepper. Ladle soup into bowls and top with dollops of herbed yogurt. Serve with warm pita bread.

Serves 4

Wine Suggestions

Morocco has produced wines for thousands of years, so the flavorings in these recipes will be quite delicious with a glass or two.

Mint, citrus, and spice are quite harmonious with Pinot Noir, so enjoy the carrots and the lamb meatballs with this popular wine. Lentil soup pairs well with Chardonnay but try it with a dry Fino sherry for something truly stupendous!

SPICED GROUND LAMB WITH YOGURT SAUCE

This recipe is equally delicious with ground beef or turkey. Use Greek-style yogurt in the sauce if you can, it will be much creamier.

  1 cup plain nonfat yogurt

  ½ cup diced English cucumber, peeled and seeded

  2 tablespoons fresh lemon juice

  2 tablespoons minced fresh mint leaves

  Salt (preferably kosher or sea salt) and freshly ground pepper

  1 pound ground lamb

  ⅓ pound ground pork

  ½ medium onion cut into ¼-inch dice

  1 tablespoon *Mystic Moroccan Herb Rub*

  1 red bell pepper, seeds and ribs removed, cut into long strips

  8 large pita rounds, cut in half

Preheat the broiler. For the sauce, mix together the yogurt, cucumber, lemon juice, and mint in a medium bowl. Season to taste with salt and pepper. Set aside.

In a large bowl, mix together the meats, onion, and *Mystic Moroccan Herb Rub*. Season with a couple pinches of salt and pepper. Form the mixture into 24 balls the size of golf balls (about 1½ inch diameter). Place

on a broiler rack and broil until cooked through, about 4 minutes per side for a total of 8 minutes. To serve, place the pitas, spiced lamb balls, and red peppers on a large platter with the bowl of yogurt sauce.

Serves 4

Napa Valley Meritage Herb Rub

INSPIRED BY THE HERBS IN THE NAPA VALLEY, THIS RUB INCLUDES LAVENDER AND ROSEMARY—A GORGEOUS COMBINATION FOR FLAVORING LAMB, PORK, CHICKEN, SALMON, AND BEEF. WE LOVE THIS RUB IN AND ON ALMOST EVERYTHING!

Rubbed & Roasted Tomatoes

6-8 medium-sized tomatoes

2 tablespoons extra-virgin olive oil

1½ tablespoons *Napa Valley Meritage Herb Rub*

Preheat the oven to 200°F. Cut the tomatoes in half or into ½-inch-thick slices if using larger tomatoes. Place on a baking sheet lined with foil or parchment paper, cut side up and drizzle olive oil over each tomato. Sprinkle with a pinch of *Napa Valley Meritage Herb Rub*. Place in the oven to roast slowly until very soft and lightly charred, approximately 3 hours, checking every hour to make sure tomatoes are roasting evenly. Smaller tomatoes will cook faster than the larger ones.

Serve at room temperature as an accompaniment to grilled meats, poultry, or fish, or as a topping on focaccia or pizza. (Roasted tomatoes can be made several days in advance and stored in the refrigerator.)

Serves 4-6

Scrambled Eggs with Herbs & Goat Cheese

I think you will agree that these are probably the best scrambled eggs you've ever had. I don't save this recipe for the weekend; it makes a quick, easy breakfast any day of the week.

2 tablespoons butter

6 large eggs

1 tablespoon *Napa Valley Meritage Herb Rub*

2 tablespoons water

¼ cup half-and-half (whole, lowfat, or nonfat milk can be substitued)

One 4-to-5-ounce log of goat cheese, crumbled

Melt the butter in a large, heavy sauté pan over medium-high heat. Combine the eggs, *Napa Valley Meritage Herb Rub*, water, and half-and-half in a large bowl and mix well. Pour the egg mixture into the sauté pan, stirring frequently. When the eggs are just starting to set, add the goat cheese and stir a couple of times to mix. Cook just until the eggs are set. Serve immediately with toasted sourdough bread, fresh fruit, and some mimosas for a festive brunch.

Serves 2-3

GRILLED LAMB CHOPS WITH HERB RUB

This is one of my favorite dishes ever. And if you don't have time to do the garlic, balsamic, and olive oil, just throw the rub on the chops and grill—delicious!

   2 cloves garlic, minced

   2 tablespoons balsamic vinegar

   2 tablespoons olive oil

   2 tablespoons *Napa Valley Meritage Herb Rub*

   8-12 boneless lamb chops, about 2 pounds

   Salt (preferably kosher or sea salt) and freshly ground pepper

   Mint or rosemary sprigs, for garnish

In a small bowl, combine the garlic, balsamic, olive oil, and *Napa Valley Meritage Herb Rub* to form a paste. Rub the paste over both sides of the lamb chops, cover, and refrigerate for at least 1 hour.

Prepare the grill. Grill the chops for 3-5 minutes per side. Season with salt and pepper to taste. Garnish with fresh mint or rosemary sprigs. Serve with Mediterranean Roasted Potatoes (page 88) and Green Beans with Mustard Dressing (page 135).

Serves 4

※

GRILLED CHICKEN WITH HERB RUB

Of course you can cook this chicken in the oven at high heat or on a gas grill, but cooking with briquettes or wood is really the way to go. I love using mesquite or oak if it is around. That is the smell you get when driving up to Mustard's restaurant in Oakville!

   1 whole chicken, about 3½ pounds (preferably free-range)

   Salt (preferably kosher or sea salt) and freshly ground pepper

   ½ cup olive oil

   ¼ cup balsamic vinegar

   ¼ cup *Napa Valley Meritage Herb Rub*

Rinse and dry the chicken, including the cavity, and season all over with salt and pepper, including the cavity. Whisk together the oil, vinegar, and *Napa Valley Meritage Herb Rub*. Place the chicken in a ziplock bag and pour the olive oil marinade over it. Close the bag and shake and massage it so the chicken is completely covered with marinade, including the cavity. The chicken can be grilled immediately but is noticeably better if you allow it to marinate for a couple of hours or overnight in the refrigerator.

Light approximately 55-60 charcoal briquettes. When they are covered with a light gray ash, separate the pile in half and move each pile to opposite sides of the grill. Put cooking grate in place and place chicken in the middle. Cover the grill, making sure the top and bottom vents are completely open. After an hour, check the chicken with a meat thermometer inserted into the fleshy part of the thigh: when it registers 170°F the chicken is done—usually between 1 and 1½ hours. Remove from grill, tent loosely with foil, and allow to rest for 10 minutes before carving.

Serves 4

Wine Suggestions

The savory herbs in this rub and the accompanying recipes will marry beautifully with a young, juicy Pinot Noir from California, Oregon, or Washington. A Grenache-based red such as Côtes du Rhône from France is another excellent choice if you are looking for an old-world wine.

A dry, un-oaked white wine made from Sauvignon Blanc or Viognier will also be magical.

SPICY AMERICAN BARBECUE HERB RUB

Don't let the term "spicy" in the name of this rub alarm you. Cumin, chipotle chile, garlic, tomato, and mustard combine to give it a little kick to wake up your taste buds. An excellent seasoning for steaks, burgers, vegetables, and sour cream dips, it's also good on potatoes—fried, baked, or in salads.

✳

SPICY HERB BUTTER

2 tablespoons *Spicy American Barbecue Herb Rub*

1 stick (½ cup) unsalted butter, room temperature

Mix both ingredients together in a food processor or small bowl. On a sheet of plastic wrap, place the butter in a rectangle about 6 x 2 inches. Roll it into a log and twist each end. Place in freezer for about 45 minutes, it should be somewhat solid. To serve, remove wrap, and slice into 1-inch coins (run knife under hot water for easy slicing).

Place a coin on the steak of your choice that has just come off the grill or out of the pan! (Store in the refrigerator for up to 6 weeks and in the freezer for up to 9 weeks.)

Serves 6

NEW YORK STRIP STEAKS WITH SEARED TOMATO VINAIGRETTE

The combination of mint and tomatoes is one of my favorites, and drizzled over a New York strip steak, what's not to like? You can use any cut of beef that you like.

> 2 tablespoons balsamic vinegar
> ¼ cup olive oil
> Salt (preferably kosher or sea salt) and fresh ground pepper
> 2 tablespoons *Spicy American Barbecue Herb Rub*
> 1 large tomato, halved
> 2 pounds New York strip steak
> 3 tablespoons minced fresh mint leaves

Prepare the grill. In a small bowl, whisk together the balsamic vinegar, 2 tablespoons of the olive oil, and a pinch of salt and set aside. In a medium bowl, combine the remaining 2 tablespoons of olive oil and the *Spicy American Barbecue Herb Rub* to form a paste. Remove ½ teaspoon of the paste and rub it onto the cut sides of the tomato and set aside. Rub the remaining paste on both sides of the steaks, coating generously. Place the steaks and tomato halves (cut sides up) on the grill. When the tomatoes are seared on the bottom and are softening, turn them over and cook 1 minute more. Transfer them to a cutting board. When the juices begin to appear on the surface of the steaks (after about 5 minutes) turn to sear the other side for another 5 minutes. Test for doneness by cutting into one of the steaks. Transfer to a platter.

Dice the tomato halves and add to the vinaigrette with the juices and the mint. Whisk to incorporate the olive oil, adding a pinch of salt and pepper. Spoon the tomato-mint vinaigrette over the steaks and serve.

Note: You can also broil the steaks. Place them on a foil-lined baking sheet and follow the same instructions as grilling for the remainder of the recipe.

Serves 4

FLANK STEAK WITH A MUSTARD RUB

So simple yet so flavorful, here's an idea, make two flank steaks at the same time, and save one for later in the week. Then you can make steak sandwiches or fajitas in about five minutes. Bonus!

⅓ cup mustard (*Herb Dijon, Hot Sweet* or your favorite)

¼ cup *Spicy American Barbecue Herb Rub*

2 pounds flank steak

Salt (preferably kosher or sea salt) and freshly ground pepper

Prepare the grill. In a small bowl, combine the mustard and *Spicy American Barbecue Herb Rub* to form a paste. Sprinkle both sides of the steaks with salt and pepper. Place the steaks on a foil-lined baking sheet and rub with the mustard paste, covering both sides with a generous amount. Let marinate for 30 minutes to 1 hour.

Place the steaks on the grill, and sear, turning to get a nice brown crust on both sides, about 5 minutes. Cook for another 6-8 minutes, turning every couple of minutes. Check for doneness by cutting into the thickest part of the steak, which should be pink in the center for medium rare. Transfer to a cutting board and cover with aluminum foil for 5 minutes before slicing on the diagonal and serving.

Serves 4

Wine Suggestions

This rub features a great combination of flavors that will take you back to your potato-chip-eating days. Smoky, spicy and yummy—pair with the same in wines!
The burgers are made for a red Rhône-style blend, while the New York strip steaks will be tasty down under with a dark, juicy Shiraz. Flank steak is one to pair with a Cabernet from your cellar—rich, ripe and powerful!

ASSORTED MINI BURGERS

Everyone loves burgers and with the minis, you can eat more than just one! Serve with your favorite condiments.

1 sourdough baguette (a round cylinder shape)

2 tablespoons olive oil

½ medium red onion, sliced very thin

1 pound extra-lean ground round

2 tablespoons *Spicy American Barbecue Herb Rub*

¼ cup shredded smoked aged cheddar cheese

2 pieces smoked bacon, cooked until crisp and crumbled

¼ cup crumbled Gorgonzola cheese

Cut the baguette into 16 quarter-inch-thick rounds. Brush with oil and toast, just until light golden and still pliable. Cook the onion in 1 tablespoon of olive oil until very soft and caramelized, about 20 minutes.

Preheat the broiler. Combine the ground beef with the *Spicy American Barbecue Herb Rub*, salt and pepper to taste, and mix well. Divide the meat mixture into 16 balls and flatten into thin patties. Place on a baking sheet and broil until cooked to your liking (a couple of minutes if you like your meat more rare.)

To assemble: place burgers on the baguette slices. Top 8 with equal parts cheddar and a sprinkle of bacon crumbles; top the remaining burgers with the onions and Gorgonzola. Place in oven and broil until cheese melts. Serve on a platter.

Makes 16 mini burgers for appetizers

Vegetables

A COLORFUL ASSORTMENT
OF VEGETABLES AND HERBS
AWAITING THE
CREATIVITY OF THE COOK

CHAPTER 8

Savory Sauces

ARTICHOKE FENNEL SAVORY SAUCE WITH CHARDONNAY

Artichoke Fennel Broth with Halibut

Summer Minestrone with Crostini

Easy Pasta Alfredo

Chicken Tagine

PUTTANESCA SAVORY SAUCE WITH CABERNET

Baked Polenta with Puttanesca Sauce

California Shellfish Stew

Manicotti Puttanesca

Fish Baked with Tomatoes, Olives & Capers

EGGPLANT BALSAMIC SAVORY SAUCE WITH MERLOT

Pizza Bread

Chicken with Eggplant Sauce over Polenta

Baked Pasta

Grilled Eggplant Parmesan Rounds

SOUTHWEST SAVORY SAUCE WITH CHARDONNAY

Zippy Zesty Gazpacho

Not Just Any Nachos

Black Bean & Sweet Potato Pozole

Southwest Stuffed Chile Peppers

WILD MUSHROOM SAVORY SAUCE WITH MERLOT

Tortellini in Mushroom-Tomato Sauce

Roasted Vegetable Lasagna

Grilled Filet Mignon with Wild Mushroom Sauce

Wild Mushroom Soup with Horseradish Cream Sauce

JANE!

ARTICHOKE FENNEL SAVORY SAUCE WITH CHARDONNAY

Chunks of artichoke and fennel mix with tomatoes in this flavor-packed sauce. It's so versatile—use with pasta and as a soup base, or reduce it down for stuffing ravioli, or on crostini with a little cheese. Or layer it with vegetables and cheese, and bake for a side dish.

✠

ARTICHOKE FENNEL BROTH WITH HALIBUT

1½ cups *Artichoke Fennel Savory Sauce with Chardonnay*

1 cup clam juice or vegetable broth

Four 4-5 ounce halibut fillets

Salt (preferably kosher or sea salt)

In a large skillet over medium-high heat, combine the *Artichoke Fennel Savory Sauce with Chardonnay* and the clam juice and bring to a simmer.

Season the halibut fillets with a pinch of salt on both sides and add to the pan. Spoon the sauce over the halibut, cover, and cook over medium heat, simmering gently until the fish is just cooked through, about 5-7 minutes depending on the thickness of the fish.

To serve, place a piece of halibut in each of four bowls and ladle the broth over the top.

Serves 4

SUMMER MINESTRONE WITH CROSTINI

I know the recipe title says "summer" but you can make this soup all year round. In the summer I serve this as starter course because it's light and refreshing. In the winter I serve it hot with a mixed field green salad for a satisfying healthy meal!

1 tablespoon olive oil

2 small carrots, peeled and cut into ¼-inch dice

2 small zucchini, cut into ¼-inch dice

1 cup thinly sliced sugar snap peas

One 26-ounce jar *Artichoke Fennel Savory Sauce with Chardonnay*

1½ cups water

8 slices baguette bread, brushed with olive oil and grilled

Extra-virgin olive oil for drizzling

Grated Parmesan cheese

Heat the olive oil in a large saucepan over medium-high heat. Add the carrots, zucchini, and peas and sauté until softened, about 5 minutes, stirring frequently. Add the *Artichoke Fennel Savory Sauce with Chardonnay* and water to the vegetables and bring to a boil. Reduce heat to a simmer and cook uncovered for 5 minutes. Taste and season with salt and pepper if necessary. Let soup cool to room temperature. Ladle into small bowls or cups and insert a baguette slice so that the top of it peeks above the rim of the cup. Serve as a starter course.

Variation: To serve warm, place a couple pieces of grilled bread in the bottom of each of four shallow soup bowls. Ladle the soup over the bread and finish with a drizzle of extra-virgin olive oil and some grated Parmesan cheese.

Serves 8 as a starter or 4 as a soup entrée

EASY PASTA ALFREDO

The combination of tomatoes and cream is just a natural. It's definitely one of the richer pastas we have, but once in a while it's okay to splurge. You know what they say, everything in moderation!

> 8 ounces dry linguine
>
> One 26-ounce jar *Artichoke Fennel Savory Sauce with Chardonnay*
>
> 1 cup half-and-half
>
> ¼ cup grated Parmesan or Asiago cheese
>
> Sea salt

Prepare the pasta according to package instructions. While pasta is cooking, heat the *Artichoke Fennel Savory Sauce with Chardonnay* in a saucepan over high heat until reduced by one-third. The sauce should be very thick. Stir in the half-and-half, mixing thoroughly. Once the pasta is cooked, drain and place in a heated bowl. Toss with sauce, finish with the grated cheese and a sprinkle of salt and serve immediately.

Serves 4

CHICKEN TAGINE

Don't you just love the fact that you open up a jar of sauce that is healthy and delicious, pour it over some chicken, go away for an hour, and come back and you have something that is very exotic and tastes really good? It is almost embarrassing!

> 4 bone-in chicken breast halves or 8 thighs
>
> Salt (preferably kosher or sea salt) and freshly ground pepper
>
> One 26 ounce jar *Artichoke Fennel Savory Sauce with Chardonnay*
>
> Fennel sprigs, for garnish (optional)

Preheat the oven to 400°F. Season the chicken with salt and pepper and place in a 13 x 9-inch baking dish. Pour *Artichoke Fennel Savory Sauce with Chardonnay* over the chicken. Cover and bake for 1 hour or until chicken is done. Serve the tagine over couscous or polenta. Garnish with fennel sprigs if desired.

Serves 4 as an entrée

Wine Suggestions

Fennel is one of the vegetable kingdoms' great accomplishments. Its licorice herbal notes are ideal with all kinds of wine. For example, the halibut dish or minestrone are made for pairing with a light Italian Pinot Grigio. The Alfredo calls for a savory red like Chianti or Sangiovese. When serving the chicken tagine, try a red Zinfandel.

EGGPLANT BALSAMIC SAVORY SAUCE WITH MERLOT

THICK, CHUNKY, AND LOADED WITH FABULOUS FLAVOR, THIS SAUCE IS MEATY LIKE A BOLOGNESE SAUCE BUT HAS NO MEAT. VEGETARIANS WILL LOVE ALL THE POSSIBILITIES—MEATLESS PASTAS, BAKED VEGETABLE DISHES, EVEN STEWS MADE WITH TOFU AND BEANS. NON-VEGETARIANS WILL LOVE IT ALSO—YOU WON'T MISS THE MEAT!

PIZZA BREAD

2 cups *Eggplant Balsamic Savory Sauce with Merlot*

1 baguette, cut in half horizontally

1 cup shredded cheese

Preheat the broiler. In a heavy saucepan, bring the *Eggplant Balsamic Savory Sauce with Merlot* to a boil over medium-high heat. Boil until sauce is very thick and reduced by about half. Place baguette on a baking sheet crust side down. Spread the sauce on the baguette then sprinkle with the cheese.

Place under the broiler until cheese bubbles. Remove from the oven, let sit until it is cool enough to touch, cut into 2-inch slices and serve immediately.

Serves 8 as an appetizer

CHICKEN WITH EGGPLANT SAUCE OVER POLENTA

This sauce tastes like it took all day to make, but no one needs to know that you just opened a jar! The flavors with the chicken and the polenta are incredible.

2 cups packaged polenta

6 boneless, skinless chicken breast halves

Salt (preferably kosher or sea salt) and freshly ground pepper

Olive oil

2 cups *Eggplant Balsamic Savory Sauce with Merlot*

Preheat the oven to 400°F. Place the chicken breasts in a bowl and add some salt and pepper and olive oil to coat them, then place chicken on a rack in a roasting pan. Bake chicken until done, usually about 15 minutes, depending on size of chicken breasts.

While chicken is baking, prepare the polenta according to package instructions.

Heat the *Eggplant Balsamic Savory Sauce with Merlot* in a saucepan and bring to a simmer. Remove chicken from oven. Place a scoop of warm polenta on each plate, top with a chicken breast and spoon about ⅓ cup of the *Savory Sauce* over the top.

Serves 6

BAKED PASTA

There is room for a lot of variation in this dish. Try using ground turkey seasoned with Poultry Herb Rub. Any ground or diced meat will work, or add more grilled or roasted vegetables for a vegetarian version.

> 1 pound of your favorite pasta
>
> 1 cup grated or shredded Parmesan cheese
>
> 4 cups shredded mozzarella cheese
>
> 2 cups *Eggplant Balsamic Savory Sauce with Merlot*
>
> 1 pound meat, cooked and drained
>
> 2 cups grilled or roasted vegetables

Preheat the oven to 350°F. Prepare the pasta according to package instructions. Mix the Parmesan and mozzarella in a bowl. In a well-greased 13 x 9-inch baking dish, spoon a thin layer of the *Eggplant Balsamic Savory Sauce with Merlot*. Build the dish in thin layers in the following order: half the pasta, half the meat, half the cheese, half the vegetables, a layer of sauce, then the remaining pasta, meat, vegetables, sauce and cheese. Cover dish with foil and bake for 25 minutes. Let stand for 15 minutes before serving. (This dish can be made ahead, covered, and refrigerated. Bring to room temperature before reheating in oven.)

Serves 4-6

This rich, almost meaty sauce is ideal with a wide variety of medium-to-full-bodied red wines.
Pair the chicken and polenta with a glass of Barbera from Piedmont or California. The grilled eggplant will be even more delicious with a Nero d'Avola from southern Italy.
Baked pasta?
Serve with a Napa Valley Merlot for true pairing pleasure!

GRILLED EGGPLANT PARMESAN ROUNDS

This sauce tastes like a bolognese sauce without the meat and is a great dish to make for your family and friends who don't eat meat. Serve as a main course or as a side to grilled chicken for those who do. I love the presentation too!

> 1½ cups *Eggplant Balsamic Savory Sauce with Merlot*
>
> 1 medium eggplant (about 1 pound), cut into eight ½-inch-thick rounds
>
> Olive oil
>
> 1 cup grated mixed cheeses (create your favorite combination of mozzarella, Fontina, Asiago, and Parmesan)
>
> ¼ cup dry bread crumbs or panko
>
> Salt (preferably kosher or sea salt) and freshly ground pepper
>
> 8 fresh basil leaves, plus additional leaves sliced thin for garnish
>
> ¼ cup freshly grated Parmesan cheese

Heat the *Eggplant Balsamic Savory Sauce with Merlot* in a saucepan over medium-high heat until it is reduced to a thick sauce. Set aside. Combine bread crumbs, cheese, and a sprinkle of salt and pepper in a small bowl.

Prepare the grill (medium heat). Brush 1 side of the eggplant slices with olive oil and sprinkle with salt and pepper. Grill, oiled side down, until bottom side is tender and grill marks appear, about 3 minutes. Brush second side of eggplant with more oil; turn and top with a little *Savory Sauce,* and the cheese mixture. Sprinkle with Parmesan and drizzle with a little olive oil. Cover and grill until the cheese melts, about 7 minutes. Transfer eggplant slices to plates.

To serve, spoon some sauce onto four small plates, top with an eggplant slice, 2 basil leaves, another slice of eggplant and a sprinkle of sliced basil leaves. Serve as a starter course for an Italian-style meal al fresco.

Serves 4

PUTTANESCA SAVORY SAUCE WITH CABERNET

Hearty and traditional, this sauce is loaded with tomatoes, olives, capers, and Cabernet. Oh so many uses; obviously it can be tossed with pasta, but it is also great for pizza or focaccia. Cook down by one-third and serve as an accompaniment with steaks, chicken, and pork.

BAKED POLENTA WITH PUTTANESCA SAUCE

1½ cups *Puttanesca Savory Sauce with Cabernet*

One 16-ounce tube prepared polenta, cut into 9 rounds

½ cup grated Parmesan cheese

Preheat the oven to 500°F. Grease a 9 x 9-inch baking dish with olive oil and spoon a ½-inch layer of *Puttanesca Savory Sauce with Cabernet* into the dish. Lay the polenta rounds in a single layer on top of the sauce in 3 rows across. Sprinkle with the cheese and place in the oven. Bake until the cheese melts and the sauce is bubbling, about 8 to 10 minutes. Let rest for 5 minutes before serving.

Serves 4 as a side dish

CALIFORNIA SHELLFISH STEW

You are going to be amazed at how great this tastes and how fast you can put it together. It will have a complex flavor that you typically get from boiling down the wine with the tomatoes and making your own fish stock from scratch.

1 tablespoon olive oil

1 medium onion, diced

One 8-ounce bottle clam juice

One 26-ounce jar *Puttanesca Savory Sauce with Cabernet*

1 pound clams in shell, scrubbed clean

1 pound halibut or snapper, skin removed, cut into 1½-inch pieces

1 pound shrimp (21-24 count), peeled and deveined with tails left intact

¾ pound scallops (large sea scallops if you can get them), halved

¾ cup chopped parsley leaves

Salt (preferably kosher or sea salt) and freshly ground pepper

Heat the oil in a large saucepan over medium heat. Add the onions and sauté until soft, about 5 minutes. Add the clam juice and the *Puttanesca Savory Sauce with Cabernet* and bring to a boil over high heat. Reduce to a simmer. While the sauce is heating, place the clams and an inch of water in a large skillet over high heat. As the clams open, transfer them one by one with a slotted spoon to a bowl. Add the clam juices to the tomato mixture.

Five minutes before you are ready to serve, add the remaining seafood to the simmering tomato base and cook 3-5 minutes until all of the seafood is opaque. Add the clams and parsley, stir, and season with salt with pepper. Divide the shellfish stew evenly among four large soup bowls. Serve with crusty sourdough bread and an extra bowl for tossing empty clam shells.

Serves 4

MANICOTTI PUTTANESCA

My grandmother used to make this dish but it took her all day long so she made it only for special occasions. You can whip this up in no time and serve it anytime, no need to wait for a special occasion.

8 ounces manicotti, about 14 pieces

One 26-ounce jar *Puttanesca Savory Sauce with Cabernet*

1 tablespoon olive oil

25 ounces ricotta cheese

5 ounces soft fresh goat cheese

1 cup grated Parmesan cheese

3 cloves garlic, minced

Salt (preferably kosher and sea salt) and freshly ground pepper

Preheat the oven to 400°F. Cook the manicotti according to package directions and drain. Cover the bottom and the sides of a 9 x 12-inch baking dish with the olive oil and pour in a little bit of the *Puttanesca Savory Sauce with Cabernet* to cover bottom. Mix the ricotta, goat cheese, and ¾ cup of the Parmesan together with the garlic, and salt and pepper to taste.

Pipe the cheese mixture into the manicotti with either a pastry bag with a fairly large tip or a plastic bag with a whole cut at the bottom corner. Put the stuffed manicotti in the baking dish and cover with the remaining *Savory Sauce*. Cover with foil and put in the center of the oven. Bake for 20 minutes. Remove the foil, sprinkle on the remaining ¼ cup Parmesan and bake for 10 more minutes or until sauce is bubbling and cheese is melted. Serve immediately

Serves 4

FISH BAKED WITH TOMATOES, OLIVES & CAPERS

Just another example of opening a jar and pairing it with a protein for a nutritious meal with big flavor and little effort!

1 teaspoon olive oil

Four 4-5 ounce halibut, sea bass, or cod fillets

1 cup *Puttanesca Savory Sauce with Cabernet*

1 cup grated mozzarella cheese (optional)

Preheat the oven to 350°F. Grease a 9 x 13-inch glass baking dish with the olive oil. Place the fillets in a single layer in the dish and spoon the *Puttanesca Savory Sauce with Cabernet* over fish. Sprinkle with grated cheese if using, and bake for 20-25 minutes, depending on the size of fish fillets. Allow to rest for 5 minutes before serving.

Serves 4

Wine Suggestions

This is the briniest of all tomato sauces and goes beautifully with seafood. The shellfish stew is a fine example for you to sip with a rosé from Sicily or Sonoma. Baked fish is simpler but just as tasty—pair with a glass of red such as a Grenache. Mannicotti is red friendly too—pair with an earthy Sangiovese.

SOUTHWEST SAVORY SAUCE WITH CHARDONNAY

THICK WITH TOMATOES, ROASTED CORN, AND ZUCCHINI, THIS SAVORY SAUCE OFFERS A TREMENDOUS AMOUNT OF VERSATILITY AND FLAVOR TO YOUR MEAL PREPARATION. TRY IT ON ENCHILADAS, GRILLED CHICKEN OR FISH, AS A SALSA FOR TORTILLA CHIPS AND QUESADILLAS, OR AS THE BASE FOR A SOUTHWEST-INSPIRED PIZZA TOPPED WITH GOAT CHEESE.

ZIPPY ZESTY GAZPACHO

One 26-ounce jar *Southwest Savory Sauce with Chardonnay*

2½ cups tomato juice

Juice of 2 limes

1 avocado, chopped

2-3 ounces queso fresco cheese or feta

¼ cup chopped cilantro leaves

Combine the *Southwest Savory Sauce with Chardonnay*, tomato juice, and lime juice, and mix well. At this point you can chill the gazpacho for an hour or serve it room temperature. Ladle the gazpacho into four bowls and top each with some avocado, cheese, and cilantro.

Serves 4

NOT JUST ANY NACHOS

These have a little different personality than your average nachos. They were inspired by an afternoon spent listening to music on the lawn at Compadres in Yountville while enjoying a margarita and nachos. They are so good you may just want to make this your dinner like we did!

1 package dried corn husks

1 pound bag tortilla chips

½ jar *Southwest Savory Sauce with Chardonnay*

⅔ cup grated jack cheese (about 4 ounces)

⅔ cup grated cheddar cheese (about 4 ounces)

One 8-ounce can black beans, drained

4 chopped green onions (white and green parts)

2 finely chopped jalapeños

¼ cup sour cream or crème fraîche

2 avocados, cubed

3 tablespoons chopped cilantro leaves

Preheat the oven to 400°F. On a large baking sheet, place 2 corn husks overlapping to create a little basket, and continue until you have 8 baskets. Place a handful of tortilla chips on each corn husk basket. Spoon some *Southwest Savory Sauce with Chardonnay* over the chips and top with the cheeses, black beans, green onions, and jalapeños. Bake until the cheese starts to bubble, about 10 minutes. Top with sour cream, avocados, and a sprinkling of cilantro. Transfer the corn husk baskets to a large platter and serve.

Note: Alternatively the nachos can be prepared on a large ovenproof platter.

Serves 8 as an appetizer

BLACK BEAN & SWEET POTATO POZOLE

This version of hominy is a vegetarian one that even a carnivore will love! It includes sweet potatoes and black beans and is wonderful served with a basket of warm cornbread.

2½ cups chicken stock

1 pound sweet potatoes, peeled and cut into ½-inch dice

One 29-ounce can hominy, drained

One 26-ounce jar *Southwest Savory Sauce with Chardonnay*

Two 15-ounce cans black beans, drained

Salt (preferably kosher or sea salt) and freshly ground pepper

1 cup shredded Monterey jack cheese

¼ cup coarsely chopped fresh cilantro leaves

4 radishes, sliced very thin

1 lime, cut into 8 wedges

In a large deep-sided pot, bring the stock to a simmer over medium-high heat. Add the potatoes and hominy; bring to a boil, reduce the heat to a simmer. Cook uncovered for 15 minutes. Add the *Southwest Savory Sauce with Chardonnay* and black beans and cook uncovered for 10 minutes more. Taste and season with salt and pepper if necessary. To serve, ladle the pozole into bowls and top with cheese, cilantro, radishes, and a squeeze of lime juice.

Variation: If you have any leftover grilled or roasted pork, dice it and add it along with the black beans.

Serves 4-6

SOUTHWEST STUFFED CHILE PEPPERS

I have been making stuffed chiles for 20 years and absolutely adore them. Once you try these, I bet you will be making them for the next 20 years. This is a great side dish with chicken or pork, or serve two for an entrée.

4 large poblano chiles

1 pound ground beef or turkey

1 clove garlic, grated

1 teaspoon cumin

Salt (preferably kosher or sea salt)

2 ounces soft fresh goat cheese log

⅓ cup grated Asiago cheese

2 cups *Southwest Savory Sauce with Chardonnay*

Preheat the oven to 400°F. Roast the chiles on the barbecue or on a gas burner until the skins are blackened all over. Remove from the grill and put in a plastic or paper bag and close the top. When cool enough to handle remove the blackened skin. Make a slit on one side of each chile (be careful not to go all the way through both sides) to create an opening. Remove the seeds and ribs. Set aside.

Heat a large skillet over medium-high heat. Add the meat, garlic, cumin, and salt to taste. Sauté until the meat is cooked through, about 7 minutes. Remove the pan from the heat and add the goat cheese, Asiago, and about ½ cup of the *Southwest Savory Sauce with Chardonnay*. Mix well. Stuff each chile with the meat mixture and then place them in a baking dish with a little water in the bottom and cover with foil. Place in the center of the oven and cook until chiles are heated all the way through, about 25-30 minutes. Heat the remaining *Savory Sauce* and spoon it over the top of the chiles.

Serves 4

Wine Suggestions

Zesty and spicy, this delicious sauce begs for an intense, lively white wine to match it stride-for-stride. Wines made from Gewürztraminer, Muscat, Riesling and Viognier have plenty of aromatic and flavor intensity to play along. Soft tannin reds (Gamay and Pinot Noir) won't clash with the spice, and reds with natural acidity (Barbera and Sangiovese) shine when paired with tomatoes.

WILD MUSHROOM SAVORY SAUCE WITH MERLOT

THE WHO'S WHO IN THE MUSHROOM WORLD—CHANTERELLES, OYSTERS, MORELS, WOOD EARS, AND PORCINIS—ARE FEATURED HERE. THIS IS A BIG, CHUNKY SAUCE THAT IS PERFECT FOR HEARTY PASTA DISHES, BUT ALSO TERRIFIC WHEN REDUCED DOWN AND USED AS A CONDIMENT FOR GRILLED MEAT AND POULTRY. TRY IT AS A SOUP ON A RAINY NIGHT.

TORTELLINI IN MUSHROOM-TOMATO SAUCE

Use whatever kind of tortellini you prefer (I like the cheese variety), and cook according to the instructions on the package.

In a separate pan, bring 2 cups of the *Wild Mushroom Sauce with Merlot* to a boil, reduce to a simmer, and cook until the sauce thickens. In a large bowl toss the tortellini with the sauce and finish with some grated cheese of your choice. Serve with some crusty bread and a glass of wine. Dinner in 10!

Serves 4

ROASTED VEGETABLE LASAGNA

One would never think a sauce that comes in a jar would be made the old-fashioned way—slowly simmered with tomatoes, Merlot, chanterelles, morels, oyster, and porcini mushrooms. That is exactly what our Wild Mushroom with Merlot Savory Sauce *is all about!*

> 8 lasagna noodles (or use fresh, which don't need cooking)
>
> 1 pound ground meat (or use roasted or grilled vegetables)
>
> One 26-ounce jar *Wild Mushroom Savory Sauce with Merlot*
>
> 2 cups shredded mozzarella cheese
>
> 2 cups ricotta cheese
>
> 1 cup grated Parmesan cheese
>
> 1 egg, lightly beaten

Cook the noodles according to the package instructions. Preheat the oven to 350°F. Brown the meat in a large skillet; drain the excess liquid. Add the *Wild Mushroom Savory Sauce with Merlot* and cook for 5 minutes. (Skip this step if you are using roasted vegetables.)

Combine the mozzarella, ricotta, ½ cup of the Parmesan cheese, and the egg in a large bowl. In a well-greased 13 x 9-inch baking dish, spread a thin layer of the meat sauce. Layer with half of the noodles, followed by half the cheese mixture, and half of the remaining meat sauce. Repeat layers and sprinkle the remaining ½ cup Parmesan cheese over the top. Cover the dish with foil and bake for 45 minutes. Remove foil and bake for 10 minutes more. Remove from oven and allow to set for 10-20 minutes before cutting and serving.

Serves 4-6

GRILLED FILET MIGNON WITH WILD MUSHROOM SAUCE

This dish reminds me of the first steak house I went to on a date. I ordered the special—a filet in a mushroom sauce with tomatoes and red wine that had some fancy name. I had no idea what I ordered but it turned out to be delicious, just like this recipe.

1½ cups *Wild Mushroom Savory Sauce with Merlot*

4 filet mignon steaks (about 1 ¾ pounds)

Salt (preferably kosher or sea salt) and freshly ground pepper

⅓ cup grated Parmesan cheese (about 2 ounces)

Prepare the grill. Heat the *Wild Mushroom Savory Sauce with Merlot* in a saucepan over medium-high heat until it is reduced to a thick sauce, and set aside.

Season the filets with salt and pepper and place on grill. When the juices begin to appear on the surface of the steaks (after about 5 minutes) turn and sear the other side for about 5 minutes more. Test for doneness by cutting into one of the steaks. Transfer to a platter. Top the steaks with the reduced *Savory Sauce* and a sprinkle of cheese. Serve with Green Beans with Mustard Dressing (page 135) and a side of orzo pasta.

Serves 4

WILD MUSHROOM SOUP WITH HORSERADISH CREAM SAUCE

½ cup crème fraîche or sour cream

2 tablespoons grated fresh horseradish, more if you like it hot

One 26-ounce jar *Wild Mushroom Savory Sauce with Merlot*

2 cups chicken, or beef stock

Sea salt to taste

In a small bowl, combine the crème fraîche and the horseradish; mix well and set aside for at least an hour to let the flavors come together. Combine the *Wild Mushroom Savory Sauce with Merlot*, and the stock in a large pot and bring to a boil. Add salt to taste. Divide the soup into four heated bowls and top with the horseradish cream.

Serves 4 as a starter

Wine Suggestions

Mushrooms have a fantastic affinity with earthy red wines such as Merlot and Pinot Noir. In addition, tomatoes are a natural with Italian varietals, especially Barbera, Nebbiolo and Sangiovese. Pour any of these wines with these dishes and you'll have a pairing that will excite the senses and brighten the meal.

Tomatoes

THE FIRST TOMATO
PLUCKED FROM THE GARDEN
OR FARMER'S MARKET
IS CAUSE FOR CELEBRATION!
WHEN THOSE TOMATOES
ARE JUST A MEMORY A SUN-DRIED
TOMATO TAPENADE IS JUST
AS DELICIOUS.

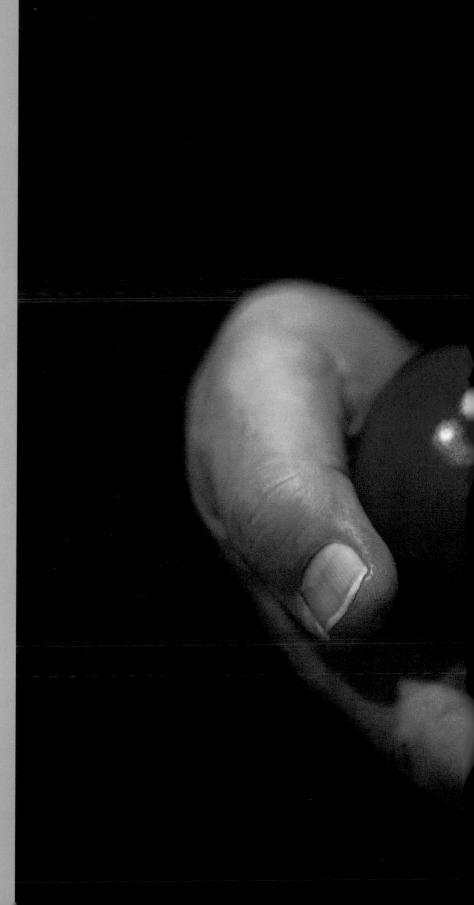

CHAPTER 9

Tapenades and Savory Condiments

FIG & ROASTED SHALLOT TAPENADE

Smoked Turkey, Goat Cheese & Fig Wraps

White Cheddar & Fig Panini

Roasted Acorn Squash with Fig & Roasted Shallots

Prosciutto & Goat Cheese Tartlets

MEDITERRANEAN TAPENADE WITH OLIVES & CAPERS

Mediterranean Appetizer Trio

Flank Steak Medallions

Grilled Tuna Niçoise Salad with Olive Tapenade

Pasta with Olives, Capers, & Goat Cheese

ROASTED TOMATO WITH BALSAMIC SAVORY CONDIMENT

Pasta Tossed with Brie, Roasted Tomatoes & Basil

Grilled Vegetable Stacks

Stuffed Zucchini

Pasta Shells Filled with Ricotta & Roasted Tomato

GREEN OLIVE WITH ROASTED TOMATO TAPENADE

Grilled Swordfish with Green Olive Tapenade

Green Olive & Roasted Tomato Tart

Hummus with a Twist

French Lentil Salad with Olives & Feta

ROASTED CORN & RED PEPPER SAVORY CONDIMENT

Chicken Fajitas

Chorizo & Roasted Corn Frittata

Roasted Corn, Red Pepper & Spiced Tortilla Scoops

Stuffed Potatoes with Roasted Corn & Red Pepper

SUN-DRIED TOMATO TAPENADE

Pizza Margherita

Sun-Drenched Risotto

Sun-Dried Tomato Mini Frittatas

White Bean & Sun-Dried Tomato Crostini

ROASTED PORTOBELLA TAPENADE WITH PORCINIS

Grilled Steaks with Mushrooms & Blue Cheese

Mushroom Potatoes au Gratin

Turkey Tenderloin with Mushroom Wine Sauce

Beef Stroganoff

JANE!®

Fig & Roasted Shallot Tapenade

So different yet so good—truly a Mediterranean delight! It's great as an accompaniment to grilled chicken or pork as well. Serve with your holiday turkey in addition to or instead of traditional cranberry sauce. Jazz up a boring turkey sandwich or spread on toasted baguette slices with some goat cheese for a fast and quite gourmet appetizer.

Smoked Turkey, Goat Cheese & Fig Wraps

4 large burrito-size flour tortillas (the thinner the better)

10 ounces fresh goat cheese, softened

¼ pound arugula leaves or fresh spinach leaves

1 pound thinly sliced smoked turkey

1 cup *Fig & Roasted Shallot Tapenade*

Spread each tortilla with one-quarter of the goat cheese. Add a single layer of arugula, leaving 2 inches around the edges uncovered. Layer with one-quarter of the turkey, spread with some *Fig & Roasted Shallot Tapenade*, and roll up. To serve as a sandwich for a picnic, cut each wrap in half on the diagonal. To serve as finger food, cut in half (not on the diagonal) and cut each half into thirds, creating 6 pinwheels per roll.

Serves 4 as picnic fare and 6-8 as part of an appetizer table

White Cheddar & Fig Panini

This is one of my favorite sandwiches. You can add a little leftover turkey if you happen to have some and that just takes it up another notch!

8 slices multigrain bread (pre-sliced, packaged bread works well)
4 teaspoons olive oil
½ cup *Fig & Roasted Shallot Tapenade*
2 cups shredded white cheddar (6 ounces)
24 basil or arugula leaves

Heat two large, heavy skillets over medium-low heat. Brush one side of each slice of bread with olive oil. Spread the other side of each slice of bread with 1 tablespoon of the *Fig & Roasted Shallot Tapenade*. Sprinkle 4 slices of the bread with half the cheese and top each with 6 basil leaves. Sprinkle the remaining cheese on top of the basil and top with the other 4 slices of bread with the tapenade side facing the cheese.

Place 2 sandwiches, oiled side down, in each skillet. Press down gently on each sandwich to condense the layers. Cook for 8-10 minutes on each side until golden brown. Repeat with remaining 2 sandwiches. Cut into quarters on the diagonal (forming 4 triangles). Serve with your favorite gourmet thick-cut chips.

Note: Low heat and slow cooking are the keys to a crunchy, evenly crisped exterior and a hot, oozing interior.

Serves 4 as a light lunch, or makes 16 mini sandwiches for an appetizer

ROASTED ACORN SQUASH WITH FIG & ROASTED SHALLOTS

My favorite time of year in the Napa Valley is fall, and this recipe reflects the season. But of course, any time is a good time to have a little Tulocay's Made in Napa Valley. We use acorn squash, but any winter squash can be substituted.

> 2 small acorn squash
>
> Olive oil (spray or liquid)
>
> Salt (preferably kosher or sea salt) and freshly ground pepper
>
> 1 teaspoon ground cinnamon
>
> 2 tablespoons brown sugar
>
> 1 cup *Fig & Roasted Shallot Tapenade*
>
> Sage or rosemary sprigs, for garnish

Preheat the oven to 400°F. Lay each squash on its side on a cutting board and slice to make ½-inch rings. Use a round biscuit or cookie cutter to remove the seeds and membrane from the center of each ring.

Spray or brush a large, foil-lined baking sheet with olive oil and arrange the rings on top. Brush squash with oil and sprinkle with salt, pepper, cinnamon, and brown sugar. Bake for 15 minutes, or until the squash is tender (the point of your knife will easily slide all the way through).

Warm the *Fig & Roasted Shallot Tapenade* in the microwave for about 30 seconds. To serve, place the slices on a platter and spoon the *Tapenade* into the center of each ring and garnish with sage or rosemary.

Serves 4

Wine Suggestions

This wonderfully satisfying fig tapenade has a hint of sweetness that will allow any dish prepared with it to pair beautifully with a rich, full-bodied white.

Think of a buttery, toasty oak Napa Valley Chardonnay, a barrel-fermented Sauvignon Blanc or Semillon, or a Gruner Veltliner from Austria for a change of pace.

PROSCIUTTO & GOAT CHEESE TARTLETS

Oh my gosh, figs, goat cheese and prosciutto in a puff pastry, what's not to like? Get them all ready to go and when your friends show up, pop them in the oven so you can serve them warm!

1 sheet (about 8-ounces) frozen puff pastry, thawed

> 5 to 6 thin slices prosciutto, cut into 1-inch squares
>
> ⅔ cup *Fig & Roasted Shallot Tapenade*
>
> 4 ounces goat cheese or feta cheese, crumbled
>
> Fresh thyme sprigs or garlic flowers

Preheat the oven to 425°F. Line 1 large or 2 small baking sheets with parchment paper or brush with oil. Unfold the puff pastry sheet (it is folded into thirds); roll out to flatten while maintaining the fold marks as guides for cutting. Cut the sheet into thirds along the fold lines, cut the three pieces in half lengthwise (you'll have 6 long strips), and then cut each of the strips into fifths for a total of 30 pieces.

Place the pastry pieces on the baking sheet about 1 inch apart. Top each pastry piece with a prosciutto square, a teaspoon of *Fig & Roasted Shallot Tapenade* and a crumble of goat cheese. Bake for 10-12 minutes until the edges are golden brown and the cheese starts to melt. Garnish with fresh thyme sprigs or garlic flowers if available.

Makes 30 individual bite-size tartlets

GREEN OLIVE WITH ROASTED TOMATO TAPENADE

GREEN OLIVES AND ROASTED TOMATOES ARE A WINNING COMBINATION. OUR TAPENADE IS SO THICK AND RICH AND JUST PLAIN GOOD THAT YOU CAN EAT IT RIGHT OUT OF THE JAR! SERVE WITH A BAGUETTE, CRACKERS, OR FLAT BREAD FOR A QUICK MUNCHIE, OR STIR INTO PASTA OR RISOTTO FOR A FAST AND FABULOUS SIDE DISH.

GRILLED SWORDFISH WITH GREEN OLIVE TAPENADE

¼ cup (or more) *Green Olive with Roasted Tomato Tapenade*

Four 4-5 ounce swordfish steaks
(or halibut, sea bass, cod, or albacore tuna)

Salt (preferably kosher or sea salt)
and freshly ground pepper

Prepare the grill. Season both sides of the fish steaks with salt and pepper before placing on hot grill. Grill for about 4 minutes per side, depending on thickness, until fish is opaque. Remove from grill and immediately top each fish steak with a spoonful of *Green Olive with Roasted Tomato Tapenade*. Serve with grilled vegetables.

Serves 4

GREEN OLIVE & ROASTED TOMATO TART

This looks so impressive and is so darn easy. Be sure and show it off before you cut it and serve it. Your guests will ooh and ah you but then when they taste it, they will applaud you.

1 sheet (about 8 ounces) frozen puff pastry, thawed

¾ cup *Green Olive with Roasted Tomato Tapenade*

⅔ cup grated fresh mozzarella (about 4 ounces)

1 pound ripe tomatoes (about 4 medium), sliced ⅛ inch thick

¼ cup grated Parmesan cheese

¼ cup fresh thyme leaves

Olive oil, for brushing

Preheat the oven to 425°F. Line a large baking sheet with aluminum foil. Unfold the puff pastry sheet and cut in half. (For individual tarts, cut the pastry into 12 rectangles.) Place the first half between 2 sheets of plastic wrap and roll out to ⅛ inch thick, maintaining the rectangular shape. Remove the top sheet of plastic wrap and turn the dough onto one side of the baking sheet and remove the remaining sheet of plastic wrap. Repeat with the other half of the puff pastry sheet. Trim any edges to even up the rectangles, if necessary. Brush the edges with water and turn over ½ inch all around. Dip the tines of a fork in flour and press them into the edges, sealing them.

Divide the *Green Olive with Roasted Tomato Tapenade* between the two rectangles and evenly spread it out to cover the pastry. Top each tart with half the mozzarella, an even layer of tomatoes (do not overlap), a sprinkling of Parmesan cheese, and thyme. Using a pastry brush, brush the edges of each tart with olive oil and place the baking sheet in the middle of the oven. Bake for 12-15 minutes until golden brown. Serve immediately. (The tarts can be made one day ahead and reheated in a 400°F oven for 5 minutes.)

Serves 6 to 8 as an appetizer or 4 with a salad as a light entrée

HUMMUS WITH A TWIST

This makes a great addition to a Greek-style meze platter with olives, feta cheese, fresh diced herbs, and fresh pita or lavosh. Your guests can assemble a pita topped with hummus, feta, and a sprinkling of fresh herbs.

1 cup *Green Olive with Roasted Tomato Tapenade*

One 15-ounce can white beans (navy, cannellini, or garbanzo beans) rinsed and drained

Paprika (smoked is wonderful if you have it)

Sprig of rosemary, parsley, or sage for garnish

1 package baked pita chips, or fresh pita bread

Combine the *Green Olive with Roasted Tomato Tapenade* and beans in a food processor and pulse, stopping to scrape down the sides as necessary. If needed add a couple of tablespoons of hot water to thin and aid in the processing until smooth. Mound in a bowl and sprinkle with paprika. Garnish with a sprig of rosemary. Serve with the pita chips, or pita bread cut into triangles.

Makes approximately 2 cups

FRENCH LENTIL SALAD WITH OLIVES & FETA

This salad reminds me of restaurant Bistro Jeanty—they don't do this exact dish but the green lentils are featured on their menu. I serve this with grilled meats and if there is any left over I roll it up in a tortilla and have it for lunch the next day!

1½ cups green lentils (or black Vertes du Puy lentils)

2 cloves garlic, lightly crushed

2 sprigs fresh thyme

4 cups water

½ cup *Green Olive with Roasted Tomato Tapenade*

Juice of 2 lemons

2 green onions (white and green parts) sliced thin on the diagonal

2 ounces crumbled feta cheese

Salt (preferable kosher or sea salt) and freshly ground pepper

1 cup cherry tomatoes, halved

Rinse the lentils and pick through, removing any stones. In a medium saucepan, combine the lentils, garlic, thyme, and water. Bring to a boil, lower heat to medium-low, partially cover, and cook 25 minutes. Check the lentils to make sure that they are firm but cooked all the way through, you do not want them mushy. Drain the lentils, remove garlic and thyme, and place in a bowl.

In a small bowl combine the *Green Olive with Roasted Tomato Tapenade*, lemon juice, and green onions to make a dressing. Stir the dressing into the warm lentils and season to taste with salt and pepper. When the lentils are room temperature, stir in the feta and tomatoes and serve. (The salad can be made one day ahead and refrigerated.) Add the cherry tomatoes right before serving.

Serves 4 to 6 as a side dish

Wine Suggestions

Green olive is a flavor found in white wines. Tomato is often found in richer red wines. Together these two make a complex match with wine.

Grilled swordfish is a match for a rich, white Rhône such as Roussanne or Viognier. The tart and hummus are made for an earthy red Rioja from Spain. Lentil salad will pair wonderfully with a dry sparkling wine like Champagne or fresh, red Beaujolais.

MEDITERRANEAN TAPENADE WITH OLIVES & CAPERS

KALAMATA OLIVES, WHOLE CAPERS, AND SWEET RED BELL PEPPERS ARE USED IN THIS TAPENADE, PROVIDING A RICH, BOLD FLAVOR. IT MAKES THE PERFECT TOPPING FOR PIZZA CRUSTS FINISHED WITH A LITTLE FETA OR GOAT CHEESE, OR IT CAN BE SPOONED ONTO BAKED OR GRILLED FISH, CHICKEN OR PORK. LITTLE EFFORT WITH BIG RESULTS ON FLAVOR!

MEDITERRANEAN APPETIZER TRIO

12 medium mushrooms, stems removed

1 cup *Mediterranean Tapenade with Olives & Capers*

12 cherry tomatoes, stemmed and seeded

2 medium cucumbers, peeled and cut into thin slices

Preheat the oven to 350°F. Fill the mushroom caps with *Mediterranean Tapenade with Olives & Capers*. Place them on a baking sheet and bake for 8-10 minutes. While mushrooms are baking, cut a small slice from the bottom of each tomato so that it will stand up. Fill the center of each tomato with the *Tapenade* — a pastry bag makes this a breeze (or use a ziplock bag with the end cut off). Spoon a little *Tapenade* onto each cucumber round. Serve the trio of appetizers on a platter or 3 separate serving dishes.

Variation: Mix softened goat cheese or whipped cream cheese with an equal amount of *Tapenade* as the filling.

Serves 6 to 8 as an appetizer

FLANK STEAK MEDALLIONS

I was doing a food demo at BV Winery and was asked what else could be made with this tapenade besides crostini? This recipe was the answer, it is super easy with unbelievable flavors.

1 pound flank steak

1 cup *Mediterranean Tapenade with Olives & Capers*

2 ounces fresh soft goat cheese, crumbled

Salt (preferably kosher or sea salt) and freshly ground pepper

Prepare the grill. Cut the steak in half and then take each half and cut in half again horizontally. You should then have 4 thin pieces. Place a piece of steak between 2 sheets of parchment or waxed paper and pound until about ¼-inch thick; repeat with remaining pieces. Sprinkle both sides of pounded flank steaks with salt and pepper and then place on a hot grill or in a hot skillet. Cook until seared on one side and turn to sear the other side, about 2 minutes per side. Do not overcook, as the meat is very thin.

Transfer the steak to a cutting board. Spread each steak with a thin layer of the *Mediterranean Tapenade with Olives & Capers* and then sprinkle with the goat cheese. Starting at the long side, roll up very tightly and place them seam side down on the cutting board pressing down a little bit. Slice each stuffed steak into three pieces and arrange the spirals on four warmed plates. Serve immediately with swiss chard or French Lentil Salad with Olives & Feta (page 119).

Serves 4

GRILLED TUNA NIÇOISE SALAD WITH OLIVE TAPENADE

I love grilled fresh tuna and it is my first choice, but if you can't find it, use canned tuna. The traditional niçoise recipe does call for canned tuna, so there you go!

¼ cup extra-virgin olive oil

¼ cup red wine vinegar

Salt (preferably kosher or sea salt) and freshly ground pepper

Four 4-5 ounce sushi-grade ahi tuna steaks

4 cups mixed salad greens

4 cups arugula

½ pound small red potatoes, boiled and cut into wedges

¼ pound green beans (preferably haricots verts), steamed

4 hard-boiled eggs, peeled and cut into 4 wedges (optional)

½ cup *Mediterranean Tapenade with Olives & Capers*

For the vinaigrette, whisk together the oil and vinegar with a pinch of salt and pepper. Set aside. Prepare the grill. Season the tuna with salt and pepper. Grill 1-2 minutes to sear the first side, then turn and sear the other side. Remove from grill.

To assemble the salad, toss together the mixed greens and arugula, lightly dress with some of the vinaigrette, and divide among four large plates. Toss the potatoes with a little vinaigrette and divide among the plates. Toss the green beans with vinaigrette and divide among the plates. Add the egg wedges to each salad around the edges. Place a grilled tuna steak in the center of each salad and top with a large spoonful of *Mediterranean Tapenade with Olives & Capers*.

Serves 4

Wine Suggestions

Earthy olive, bright caper, and a big splash of Merlot make this tapenade perfect with wine. The pasta is delicious with a southern French blend of Grenache, Mourvedre and Syrah.

Flank steak works well with a blend too, but why not try a Meritage instead? Grilled Tuna Nicoise is made for rosé or a light red such as a California Rhône-style red blend.

PASTA WITH OLIVES, CAPERS & GOAT CHEESE

Wouldn't you love a killer dish that takes as long to prepare as it takes to boil pasta? Here you go!

8 ounces dried pasta (gemelli, fusilli, penne, or orecchiette)

3 ounces fresh soft goat cheese, crumbled

1 cup *Mediterranean Tapenade with Olives & Capers*

Grated Parmesan cheese

Cook the pasta according to package instructions. Place the hot pasta in a large bowl and add the goat cheese and *Mediterranean Tapenade with Olives & Capers*. Mix well. Serve topped with grated Parmesan to taste.

Variation: Add 2 cups of diced grilled chicken and 1 cup diced roasted red peppers for a more substantial dish.

Serves 4

ROASTED CORN & RED PEPPER SAVORY CONDIMENT

SMOKY AND OH SO GOOD! THIS CONDIMENT IS DELICIOUS SERVED AS AN ACCOMPANIMENT TO GRILLED POULTRY AND MEATS. SERVE AS A SALSA FOR BURRITOS AND TACOS OR EVEN HUEVOS RANCHEROS, OR ADD TO NACHOS ALONG WITH BLACK BEANS, CHEESE, SOUR CREAM, AND GUACAMOLE. GIVE PIZZA A SOUTH-OF-THE-BORDER FLAIR WITH ROASTED CORN & RED PEPPER SAVORY CONDIMENT, GOAT CHEESE, AND A SPRINKLING OF CHOPPED CILANTRO.

CHICKEN FAJITAS

For quick and easy fajitas, use leftover grilled chicken cut into strips (or chicken tenders) and tuck into tortillas with some *Roasted Corn & Red Pepper Savory Condiment*, slices of avocado, chopped green onions, and shredded cheddar. Top with a spoonful of sour cream and chopped cilantro.

CHORIZO & ROASTED CORN FRITTATA

Is this a Mexican or an Italian dish? I don't know but it is so darn good. Feel free to make it ahead and just pop it in the oven about 40 minutes before you want to serve. It's a winner!

14 ounces chorizo sausage squeezed out of casings (or use chicken or turkey sausages)

9 large eggs

Salt (preferably kosher or sea salt) and freshly ground pepper

½ cup *Roasted Corn & Red Pepper Savory Condiment*

¼ cup half-and-half

2 tablespoons water

1 cup shredded cheese (Mexican blend, mozzarella, or your favorite melting cheese)

Preheat the oven to 375°F. Heat a 12-inch ovenproof skillet over medium-high heat, add the sausage and cook until it is no longer pink, about 7 minutes. Drain the liquid from the skillet and set aside. Beat the eggs, salt, and pepper together in a large bowl. Whisk in the *Roasted Corn & Red Pepper Savory Condiment*, half-and-half, and water.

Heat the skillet with the sausage over medium heat and pour the egg mixture over the top. Sprinkle with the cheese and cook until the frittata is just cooked around the edges, about 10 minutes. Transfer the skillet to the oven and bake until set, about 20 minutes. Remove from oven and let cool about 10 minutes before cutting into wedges and serving. A salad of mixed greens and a loaf of crusty bread are the perfect accompaniments.

Serves 4-6 as a light entrée

ROASTED CORN, RED PEPPER & SPICED TORTILLA SCOOPS

I have made literally thousands of these! You can also make this dish nacho style by putting regular tortilla chips on a platter, adding the corn and meat mixture, then finishing off with the sour cream, lime, and cilantro.

> 1 teaspoon olive oil
>
> ¼ cup finely diced onion
>
> 1 pound ground turkey (or ground beef)
>
> 1 cup *Roasted Corn & Red Pepper Savory Condiment*
>
> Pinch of salt (preferably kosher or sea salt)
>
> 3-4 tablespoons water
>
> One 12-ounce bag Tortilla Scoops
>
> ¼ cup sour cream (low fat or fat free are fine)
>
> Juice of ½ lime
>
> Cilantro leaves, for garnish

Heat the oil in a large, heavy skillet over medium-high heat. Add the onions and sauté until softened, about 3 minutes. Add the turkey, stirring to break it up as it cooks and turns opaque. The turkey will be fully cooked after 7 minutes. Add the *Roasted Corn & Red Pepper Savory Condiment* to the pan with a generous pinch of salt and mix thoroughly. Stir in the water, cook for 1 minute more, and remove from heat.

In a small bowl mix together the sour cream and lime juice. To assemble, fill each scoop with a teaspoon of turkey mixture and top with a drizzle of sour cream and a cilantro leaf.

Serves 6 to 8 as an appetizer

✳

STUFFED POTATOES WITH ROASTED CORN & RED PEPPER

Sometimes one of these potatoes with a lightly dressed salad is all you need, okay maybe a glass of vino too! For a little more flavor, add some grated cheese in the last couple of minutes of baking.

> 2 large russet potatoes, scrubbed and poked several times with a fork
>
> 1 tablespoon olive oil or butter
>
> ⅓ cup milk, half-and-half, heavy cream, or sour cream
>
> 1 teaspoon *Poultry Herb Rub* (or season to taste with kosher or sea salt)
>
> 1 cup *Roasted Corn & Red Pepper Savory Condiment*

Preheat the oven to 450°F. Bake the potatoes for about 1 hour or until tender. Let potatoes cool for a few minutes; then cut each in half lengthwise. Scoop the insides into a bowl, taking care not to break the skins. Use a fork to mash the potatoes with the olive oil, milk, and *Poultry Herb Rub*.

Fold the *Roasted Corn & Red Pepper Condiment* into the potato mixture. Spoon the filling back into the potato skins. Reduce oven to 350°F. Place the potatoes on a baking sheet and return to the oven for 15-20 minutes, until the potatoes are heated through and lightly browned on top. Serve immediately.

Serves 4

Wine Suggestions

The aromatic floral and fruity Riesling is the perfect marriage for corn, spice, and a smidge of smoke as it contrasts amazingly well. Try one from California, New York, Washington, Germany or Australia.

The recipes for this savory condiment will also absolutely resonate with a smoky oaky Pinot Noir.

ROASTED PORTOBELLA TAPENADE WITH PORCINIS

THE ROASTED RICH FLAVOR OF PORTOBELLA AND PORCINI MUSHROOMS LENDS ITSELF TO A WIDE VARIETY OF USES. STIR IT INTO A RISOTTO FOR AN ELEGANT ENTRÉE OR MAKE A DELICIOUS, CASUAL WEEKDAY PASTA SUPPER. SPOON ONTO FRESH PORTOBELLA MUSHROOM CAPS, TOP WITH BREAD CRUMBS AND GRATED CHEESE AND BAKE FOR A VEGETARIAN ENTRÉE.

GRILLED STEAKS WITH MUSHROOMS & BLUE CHEESE

To create this steak-house classic, grill the steaks (we like rib-eyes) and serve topped with the *Roasted Portobella Tapenade with Porcinis* (heat the *Tapenade* in a saucepan right before serving) and a crumble of your favorite blue cheese (we suggest a mild blue.)

The perfect accompaniments are the Spiced Potato Wedges (page 82) and a bottle of Napa Valley Cabernet Sauvignon.

124

MUSHROOM POTATOES AU GRATIN

Oh my gosh, I love potatoes au gratin all by themselves, but when you add the mushrooms, we are talking divine!

> 3 pounds russet potatoes, peeled and cut into ⅛-inch-thick slices
> 3 cups milk
> 2 cloves garlic, minced
> Salt (preferably kosher or sea salt) and freshly ground pepper
> ½ cup *Roasted Portobella Tapenade with Porcinis*
> 1 tablespoon butter
> ⅔ cup shredded Gruyére cheese (4 ounces)

Preheat the oven to 400°F. In a stockpot set over medium-high heat, combine the potatoes, milk, garlic, a couple of pinches of salt and pepper and bring to a boil. Remove from heat.

In a small sauté pan over high heat, cook the *Roasted Portobella Tapenade with Porcinis* for about 2 minutes to reduce some of the liquid. Butter a 9 x 12-inch baking dish and using a slotted spoon, place a third of the potatoes in the dish and cover the bottom. Spoon half of the *Tapenade* over the potatoes and top with half of the cheese. Place another layer of potatoes in dish topped by remaining half of *Tapenade* and then remaining potatoes. Pour the milk mixture evenly over the potatoes and *Tapenade*. Top with the remaining cheese and bake for 35 minutes or until bubbling and top is browned.

Serves 8 as a side dish

TURKEY TENDERLOIN WITH MUSHROOM WINE SAUCE

Mushrooms and red wine are a natural with steak but try this—Roasted Portobella Tapenade and white wine slathered on a turkey tenderloin. I think you will agree that this is pretty fabulous!

> 2 turkey tenderloins (about 1½ pounds) cut in half
>
> Salt (preferably kosher or sea salt) and freshly ground pepper
>
> 1 cup *Roasted Portobella Tapenade with Porcinis*
>
> ½ cup white wine of your choice (I am a Chardonnay girl)
>
> Crème fraîche or sour cream
>
> 4 sprigs oregano

Prepare the grill. Season the turkey tenderloins with salt and pepper. On the grill or in a sauté pan on the stovetop, cook the turkey tenderloins for about 6 minutes per side until cooked through.

In a medium saucepan over medium heat, combine the *Roasted Portobella Tapenade with Porcini*s and the wine and bring to a simmer.

To serve, place a turkey tenderloin on each of four plates and spoon a quarter of the sauce over each. Top with a dollop of crème fraîche and a sprig of oregano.

Serves 4

Wine Suggestions

Mushrooms are the most savory of all vegetables; also the most wine-friendly. Grilled steak is the perfect accompaniment to a fine Cabernet Sauvignon.

Beef Stroganoff is pretty darn good with very, very cold vodka; as an alternative try a rich Chardonnay or Cabernet Sauvignon. The turkey tenderloin or the potatoes are absolutely yummy with a rich red such as Merlot.

BEEF STROGANOFF

My Mom used to make the best beef stroganoff but this is a close second for sure. She always served it with the wide egg noodles but I like to use pappardelle.

> 8 ounces dried pappardelle, fettuccine, or linguine
>
> 1 to 2 tablespoons butter
>
> 1 pound beef tenderloin filet (filet mignon), cut into ⅜-inch-thick strips
>
> One 8-ounce package sliced button or cremini mushrooms
>
> 1 cup *Roasted Portobella Tapenade with Porcinis*
>
> ¼ cup sherry, preferably medium-dry
>
> 1 cup sour cream
>
> Salt (preferably kosher or sea salt) and freshly ground pepper
>
> ¼ cup chopped flat-leaf parsley or dill

Cook the pasta according to package instructions. Melt the butter in a medium-sized sauté pan over high heat. Add the beef and quickly sear on both sides, no more than a minute or two per side, remove from pan, and set aside. Reduce the heat to medium, add the mushrooms, cover, and cook until softened, about 2-3 minutes, checking to make sure the mushrooms are not drying out and sticking to pan. Add the *Roasted Portobella Tapenade with Porcinis* and the sherry. Reduce heat to low and simmer for 5 minutes. Add the beef, sour cream, and salt and pepper to taste, stirring until the sour cream is blended. Simmer just until heated through, about 5 minutes more. Serve immediately over the pasta and sprinkle with the parsley.

Serves 4

ROASTED TOMATO WITH BALSAMIC SAVORY CONDIMENT

THE ITALIANS ARE ON TO SOMETHING WITH THE COMBINATION OF TOMATOES AND BALSAMIC! WE GO ONE STEP FURTHER AND ROAST THE TOMATOES FOR ULTRA FLAVOR. IN THE DEAD OF WINTER WHEN TOMATOES ARE BLAND, SERVE THIS CONDIMENT WITH ROASTED OR GRILLED MEATS AND CHICKEN. IT'S IDEAL FOR TOPPING PIZZAS, FOCACCIA, OR BAGUETTES AND FABULOUS IN OMELETS TOO!

PASTA TOSSED WITH BRIE, ROASTED TOMATOES & BASIL

1 cup *Roasted Tomato with Balsamic Savory Condiment*

5 ounces Brie cheese, cubed

½ cup chopped fresh basil leaves

8 ounces dried penne, orecchiette, or fusilli

Grated Parmesan cheese

In a large bowl, combine the *Roasted Tomato with Balsamic Savory Condiment*, Brie, and basil; mix thoroughly.

Cook pasta according to package instructions, drain well (do not rinse). Add the hot pasta to the *Savory Condiment* mixture. Toss to combine, the brie should start melting. Serve with the cheese sprinkled on top.

Serves 4

GRILLED VEGETABLE STACKS

You can do this with just about any veggies that you happen to have and any type of cheese that melts. Try Fontina or Gruyère, you and your family will be begging for more.

4 medium (about 3 inches in diameter) portobella mushrooms, dark gills scooped out

1 red bell pepper, quartered lengthwise

1 yellow bell pepper, quartered lengthwise

4 slices medium to large zucchini, cut into rounds

4 slices medium eggplant, cut into rounds

4 slices fresh mozzarella

Olive oil

Salt (preferably kosher or sea salt) and freshly ground pepper

1 cup *Roasted Tomato with Balsamic Savory Condiment*

4 rosemary branches 4-5 inches in length, bottom two-thirds of leaves removed

Prepare the grill. Brush the vegetables with olive oil, season with salt and pepper to taste, and grill each vegetable until done. Turn each mushroom upside down on a flat surface to use as the base for the stack, then layer with a slice of yellow pepper, a slice of zucchini, red pepper, mozzarella, and eggplant.

Place the stacks back on the grill off to the side, close the lid and cook until the cheese starts to melt (alternatively the stacks can be heated in a 400°F oven for 10 minutes.) Remove from grill, then poke a rosemary sprig through the middle of each stack with the leaves at the top of the stack.

Heat the *Roasted Tomato with Balsamic Savory Condiment* in a small saucepan over medium heat. Spoon ¼ cup in a pool on each of four salad plates. Top with a vegetable stack. Serve immediately.

Serves 4 as a starter or a side to grilled meat; 4-6 as a light entrée.

STUFFED ZUCCHINI

This is one vegetable dish that I make all the time. It looks like it would be a lot of work but it literally takes only 5 minutes to prepare – zucchini and tomatoes are such a natural pairing! This is delicious served as a side dish with chicken or as part of a vegetarian meal with a salad and pasta (try the Pasta with Olives, Capers & Goat Cheese on page 121) or risotto.

4 medium zucchini cut in half lengthwise

½ cup *Roasted Tomato with Balsamic Savory Condiment*

⅓ cup grated Parmesan or Asiago Cheese

Preheat the oven to 400°F. Scoop out the center of each zucchini half with a small spoon (⅛ teaspoon works well). Fill the cavities with the *Roasted Tomato with Balsamic Savory Condiment*, top with the cheese and set into an oiled baking dish. Bake for 20 minutes. Remove and serve immediately.

Serves 4 as a side dish

PASTA SHELLS FILLED WITH RICOTTA & ROASTED TOMATO

The first time I made stuffed pasta shells, I thought it would be difficult. But to my delight it's actually quite easy and a dish that can be made ahead and reheated.

1 pound large pasta shells

15 ounces ricotta cheese

1 large egg, lightly beaten

1 cup shredded mozzarella cheese

½ cup *Roasted Tomato with Balsamic Savory Condiment*

Salt (preferably kosher or sea salt) and freshly ground pepper

1 cup chicken stock

1 cup dry red wine

One 28-ounce can crushed tomatoes

1 cup grated Parmesan cheese

Preheat the oven to 350°F. Cook the pasta according to package instructions, drain. In a large bowl combine the ricotta cheese, egg, mozzarella cheese, ¼ cup of the *Roasted Tomato with Balsamic Savory Condiment* and salt and pepper to taste. Mix well. Spoon the mixture into the shells and place in a baking dish large enough to hold the shells in a single layer.

In a medium-sized saucepan over medium-high heat, combine the chicken stock, wine, tomatoes, and the remaining ¼ cup *Savory Condiment*. Bring to a boil. Pour the sauce over the stuffed shells, and sprinkle with the Parmesan cheese. Cover the baking dish with foil and bake for 30 minutes. Serve immediately.

Serves 6-8

Wine Suggestions

Roasting tomatoes brings out their sweet earthiness. Letting grapes hang until they are rich and ripe gives a fruitful, earthy quality to red wines also.

Lush reds like Zinfandel or Grenache are just the ticket with the grilled vegetable stacks and stuffed zucchini. The pastas will both be so good with a ripe, lusty Syrah!

SUN-DRIED TOMATO TAPENADE

Vibrant with the flavor of ripe sun-warmed tomatoes, this salsa makes a scrumptious pizza with goat cheese and fresh basil. Use it to top a grilled turkey burger for a different twist on burgers. It's also dynamite blended with cream cheese for a dip with fresh vegetables and crackers.

PIZZA MARGHERITA

Pizzas are such fun to make and serve as a casual supper or an appetizer for an Italian-themed party. Of course you can use a 12-inch prepared pizza crust, but there is nothing like a pizza that starts with dough that is rolled very thin and cooked on a pizza stone in a 500°F oven.

Simply spread the dough (premade dough can be purchased from your local pizzeria or specialty grocery) with a thin layer of *Sun-Dried Tomato Tapenade*, sprinkle with shredded mozzarella cheese and bake for about 7 minutes until the crust is crisp and the cheese is bubbling. Top with chopped fresh basil leaves, slice and serve—delicioso!

Makes one 12-inch pizza

SUN-DRENCHED RISOTTO

I used to stay away from risotto because I thought it was so much work, but I have learned that it is easy and a great one pot-dish that feeds a crowd.

> 5 cups low-sodium chicken or vegetable broth
> 2 tablespoons olive oil
> ½ medium onion, finely diced
> 1½ cups Arborio rice
> ⅓ cup dry white wine
> ½ cup *Sun-Dried Tomato Tapenade*
> ⅓ cup grated Parmesan cheese

In a medium saucepan, bring the broth to a simmer and reduce the heat to low. Heat the oil in a large low-sided skillet over medium-high heat. Add the onion and sauté for 5 minutes until it softens. Add the rice, stirring to coat the grains with oil, and cook for 3 minutes until the rice begins to lose the opaque color. Add the wine and cook until it evaporates, about 3 minutes.

Now you can begin the 18-minute cooking time. Ladle enough of the hot broth over the rice to cover it, continue stirring until the broth is almost absorbed, and add more broth just to cover. Continue cooking, stirring and adding broth to the rice. After 18 minutes, bite on a kernel of rice to test for doneness. It should be al dente (cooked all the way through but still have some texture). Stir in the *Sun-Dried Tomato Tapenade* and ¼ cup of the Parmesan cheese. Serve the risotto in heated bowls sprinkled with the remaining Parmesan.

Serves 4

SUN-DRIED TOMATO MINI FRITTATAS

These are terrific served right out of the oven, but I have also taken them to outdoor events and served them at room temperature and they are always a hit. As the frittatas cool they will deflate a bit. Frittatas may be made ahead and reheated. This can be made as one large frittata as well.

8 large eggs

1 cup milk (preferably whole)

½ teaspoon salt (preferably kosher or sea salt)

½ teaspoon freshly ground pepper

¾ cup *Sun-Dried Tomato Tapenade*

⅓ cup grated Parmesan cheese

2 tablespoons chopped fresh basil leaves

Preheat the oven to 350°F. Spray a 12-cup muffin pan with oil. In a large bowl, whisk together the eggs, milk, salt, and pepper. Stir in ½ cup of the *Sun-Dried Tomato Tapenade*, the cheese, and basil. Divide the egg mixture among the muffin cups. Bake for 20-25 minutes. The frittatas will be puffed and golden brown when done. Serve topped with a spoonful of the remaining ¼ cup *Tapenade*. Serve with Heirloom Tomato Salad with Mozzarella (page 19) for a light summer supper.

Makes 12

Wine Suggestions

Tomatoes and the sun instantly make one think of the Mediterranean, so it's natural that grapes originally from this region offer the ideal match for all of these dishes.

Try a California Zinfandel or Syrah; Italian varietals (red Sangiovese and Negroamaro, or white Fiano di Avellino and Vernaccia) will work wonders; and the Spanish red Tempranillo or white Viura all will have you singing their praises.

WHITE BEAN & SUN-DRIED TOMATO CROSTINI

The addition of white beans make this a little different than your typical crostini topping. If you have any left over it is also dynamite served as a condiment with fish or chicken.

One 15-ounce can white beans (navy or cannellini) rinsed and drained

½ cup *Sun-Dried Tomato Tapenade*

8 basil leaves, stacked on one another, rolled and cut into thin strips (chiffonade), reserve 2 tablespoons for garnish

½ cup grated Parmesan cheese, reserve 2 tablespoons for garnish

Salt (preferably kosher or sea salt) and freshly ground pepper

1 baguette, thinly sliced on the diagonal and grilled or toasted

Extra-virgin olive oil

In a medium bowl, combine the beans, *Sun-Dried Tomato Tapenade*, basil, and Parmesan; mix well. Season to taste with salt and pepper. Top each baguette toast with a spoonful of the white bean mixture, a sprinkle of Parmesan and basil, and a drizzle of extra-virgin olive oil. Serve on a platter with a crock of olives, slices of salami, and wedges of cheese for an Italian-style antipasti platter.

Serves 4-6 as an appetizer

CHAPTER 10

Mustards

HERB DIJON MUSTARD WITH CHARDONNAY

Mustard-Glazed Grilled Pork Chops

Salmon Salad on Butter Lettuce

Green Beans with Mustard Dressing

Napa Valley Succotash

HOT SWEET MUSTARD WITH CHAMPAGNE

Mini Sausage Wraps with Mustard Dipping Sauces

Corn & Zucchini Tart

Grilled Portobella Sandwiches with Hot-Sweet Mustard-Mayo

Scallops in Mustard-Wine Sauce

STONE GROUND MUSTARD WITH CABERNET

Enlightened Mustard Cream Sauce

Mediterranean Potato Salad

Prosciutto Rolls

Eggs Napa with Spinach & Mustard Sauce

JANE!

HERB DIJON MUSTARD WITH CHARDONNAY

Gold Medal Winner at the 2002 Napa Valley Mustard Festival, our proprietary herb blend is added to a traditional Dijon-style mustard along with Chardonnay. Create a savory vinaigrette for butter lettuce salads or potato and pasta salads. This mustard makes an ordinary sandwich extraordinary.

MUSTARD-GLAZED GRILLED PORK CHOPS

Four 8-10 ounce loin pork chops, bone in (or center-cut, boneless pork loin)

⅓ cup *Herb Dijon Mustard with Chardonnay*

Salt (preferably kosher or sea salt)

Prepare the grill. Season the pork chops with salt and pepper and coat with *Herb Dijon Mustard with Chardonnay*. Depending on the heat of the grill and thickness of chops, grill the chops for 4-5 minutes per side. Check for doneness by making a small cut in the center of the chop, which should be barely pink.

Serves 4

SALMON SALAD ON BUTTER LETTUCE

This is one of my favorite lunches to bring to work. I add a little dressing to the salmon mixture and then wrap it in the lettuce leaves like a burrito and eat it on the go! It's healthy and delicious.

- 2 teaspoons minced fresh tarragon
- 1 clove garlic, minced
- 2 tablespoons Champagne vinegar (or white wine vinegar)
- 1 tablespoon *Herb Dijon Mustard with Chardonnay*
- ½ teaspoon salt (preferably kosher or sea salt)
- ⅔ cup extra-virgin olive oil
- ¾ pound fresh cooked salmon (canned salmon or albacore tuna can be substituted)
- 3 green onions (white and green parts) chopped
- 1 roasted red bell pepper, cut into thin strips
- 2 heads butter lettuce

To prepare the dressing, combine the tarragon, garlic, vinegar, *Herb Dijon Mustard with Chardonnay* and salt in a small mixing bowl or 2 cup measuring cup. Gradually whisk in the olive oil until thickened and thoroughly blended. Refrigerate for at least an hour.

In a medium-sized bowl combine the fish, green onions, and red peppers. Gently mix together, trying not to break up the fish too much. On each of 4 chilled plates, place 3 lettuce leaves overlapping to form a cup. Divide the fish mixture evenly among the plates, drizzle with dressing and serve! A nice touch is to serve with chilled forks.

Serves 4 as a light lunch

GREEN BEANS WITH MUSTARD DRESSING

Remember the green bean casserole with the dry onion soup mix served at holiday meals? We suggest you bring this dish instead for a contemporary green bean side dish — you'll get rave reviews. It is also a great starter course or side dish for any meal, any time of year.

¾ pound haricots verts (thin tender green beans) or try asparagus spears

2 tablespoons unsalted butter

2 tablespoons minced shallots

1 cup chicken stock

3 tablespoons heavy cream

2 tablespoons *Herb Dijon Mustard with Chardonnay*

Salt (preferably kosher or sea salt) and freshly ground pepper

Bring a saucepan of water to a boil, and add the beans. Reduce the heat and simmer for 3-5 minutes. Drain, rinse under cold water, and pat dry. Set aside.

Melt the butter over medium heat in a medium saucepan. Add the shallots and sauté for 3 minutes over medium heat. Stir in the stock, cream, and *Herb Dijon Mustard with Chardonnay* and cook until the mixture is just slightly thickened, 5 minutes or so. Then add the beans and toss them in the sauce until well coated and heated through, 2-3 minutes.

Season with salt and pepper and serve immediately.

Serves 4 to 6

NAPA VALLEY SUCCOTASH

A twist on the traditional Southwestern succotash made with lima beans, this is a great way to get people to eat their veggies. It's a tasty accompaniment to grilled lamb chops—steak, chicken, or fish too!

6 tablespoons olive oil

1 large onion, diced

3 zucchini, quartered and chopped

2 ears white or yellow corn, cut from cob

1 large red bell pepper, roasted, peeled, and chopped

½ cup chopped cilantro leaves

2 tablespoons *Herb Dijon Mustard with Chardonnay*

8 lamb chops (optional if you just want to make the succotash)

In a large sauté pan, heat 2 tablespoons of the oil over medium heat. Add the onions and sauté until they begin to soften, about 5 minutes. Add the zucchini and corn and continue to cook until vegetables are shiny, about 3 minutes. Reduce the heat and add the roasted peppers. Mix together the remaining 4 tablespoons of olive oil with the *Herb Dijon Mustard with Chardonnay* and pour half into the vegetables. Toss well and cook until veggies are cooked all the way through, about 2 minutes more. Stir in the cilantro.

If serving the lamb, prepare the grill and season the chops with salt and pepper. Grill the chops to desired doneness. Divide the vegetables among four plates, top with 2 chops, and then drizzle with some of the remaining mustard sauce. Serve immediately.

Serves 4

Wine Suggestions

Dijon-style mustard is Chardonnay-friendly as the name implies. The pork chops have a sweet meaty flavor and mustardy bite to pair wonderfully with a crisp Chardonnay. A richer, tropical style of Chardonnay is a delight with the green beans or the succotash.
For the salmon salad try a lighter grape such as Sauvignon Blanc or Pinot Gris.

WE COMBINED SPARKLING WINE AND SHALLOTS TO GIVE THIS MUSTARD A SOFT AND ELEGANT TASTE. IT IS TERRIFIC AS A SPREAD ON SANDWICHES OR SERVED WITH ALL TYPES OF SAUSAGES. THE HOT-SWEET COMBINATION IS FANTASTIC AS A GLAZE FOR A HAM AS WELL.

MINI SAUSAGE WRAPS WITH MUSTARD DIPPING SAUCES

1 sheet (about 8 ounces) frozen puff pastry, thawed

16 mini sausages (turkey and apple, or your favorite variety)

½ cup *Hot Sweet Mustard with Champagne*

2 tablespoons balsamic vinegar

2 tablespoons maple syrup

Preheat the oven to 375°F. Unfold the pastry sheet. Cut along one fold and save that piece. Rewrap the remaining two-thirds of the sheet for another use. Cut the dough into 8 equal rectangles and cut each rectangle in half diagonally, forming 16 triangles. Wrap each sausage with a pastry triangle starting with the sausage at the wide end of the triangle and roll it up. Place sausages on a baking sheet and bake for 15-18 minutes or until golden.

For the sauces: combine ¼ cup *Hot Sweet Mustard with Champagne* and the balsamic for one and the remaining ¼ cup *Mustard* with the maple syrup for the other.

Makes 16 appetizers

CORN & ZUCCHINI TART

This is a little more work than most of our recipes, but definitely worth it. Have you ever had a crust made out of zucchini and then complemented with a corn and cheese filling? You will love it!

4 medium zucchini, coarsely shredded (about 4 cups)

1 teaspoon salt (preferably kosher or sea salt)

1 large egg, lightly beaten

3 tablespoons *Hot Sweet Mustard with Champagne*

¾ cup cornmeal

1 tablespoon olive oil

½ cup minced red onion

1 cup corn kernels cut from cob

¼ cup chopped fresh basil leaves (or fresh herb of your choice)

1 large tomato, seeded and cut into ¼-inch dice

1 cup shredded Fontina cheese

2 tablespoons grated Parmesan cheese

Preheat the oven to 375°F. To make the crust, toss the zucchini with the salt and drain in a colander for 30 minutes. Squeeze the excess water from the zucchini. Combine the zucchini with the egg and *Hot Sweet Mustard with Champagne*. Press into an oiled 9-inch pie plate. Bake for 20 minutes.

While the crust is baking, prepare the filling. Heat the oil in a large skillet over medium-high heat. Sauté the onions and corn until the onions begin to soften, about 5 minutes. Place the corn mixture in a medium bowl and cool slightly. Add the basil, tomato, and Fontina and mix thoroughly. Pour the filling evenly in the pie crust. Top with the Parmesan cheese and bake for 20-25 minutes. Let sit 5-10 minutes prior to cutting into wedges and serving.

Serves 4-6 as a light entrée

Grilled Portobella Sandwiches with Hot Sweet Mustard-Mayo

We can't eat burgers seven days a week or at least we probably shouldn't. So when in the mood for a burger, try this instead. The ultimate veggie burger in my book!

4 large portobella mushrooms, wiped clean with damp cloth
Leaves from sprig of fresh rosemary
¼ cup olive oil
1 large tomato, cut crosswise into ½-inch slices
Salt (preferably kosher or sea salt) and freshly ground pepper
Six 4-inch squares focaccia, or three 5-inch sections fresh baguette, split
1 bunch arugula
2 tablespoons *Hot Sweet Mustard with Champagne*
2 tablespoons mayonnaise

Prepare the grill. Cut the stems off the mushrooms flush with the caps. Combine the oil with the rosemary and place in the mushroom caps. Marinate for 30 minutes if you have time. Brush tomato slices with the same mixture and season with salt and pepper to taste.

Mix the *Hot Sweet Mustard with Champagne* and the mayonnaise together and set aside. Grill the mushrooms and tomato slices for about 4 minutes each side. Lightly toast the focaccia on the grill.

To assemble: Spread one side of each focaccia slice with the mustard mayo, and place a grilled mushroom on each. Add the tomato and arugula, and top with remaining focaccia slices.

Makes 4 sandwiches

Wine Suggestions

Of course, a sparkling wine or Champagne would be a match made in heaven for these mustard dishes. Select one labeled Brut (dry) or Extra-Dry (not as dry as Brut).

If you aren't in the mood for bubbles, try a refreshing Riesling from Germany, California, or Washington state, one that is dry or finished with a kiss of sweetness to tame the zing of the mustard.

Scallops in Mustard-Wine Sauce

I used to think that a dish with a sauce like this was one that you had only at restaurant, prepared by a chef. I found that you don't need to be a trained professional chef to make this at home but you'll look like one when you serve it!

1 pound sea scallops (or day boat scallops if available)
Salt (preferably kosher or sea salt) and freshly ground pepper
1 tablespoon olive oil
⅓ cup white wine
½ cup water
3 tablespoons *Hot Sweet Mustard with Champagne*
2 tablespoons unsalted butter, at room temperature
4 cups arugula
Chopped fresh herbs, for garnish (basil, tarragon, mint, or Italian parsley)

Pat the scallops dry and season with salt and pepper. Heat the oil in a large skillet over medium-high heat. Add the scallops and sauté until golden and cooked through, about 2 minutes per side. Transfer to a plate and loosely cover with foil. Add the wine and simmer over medium-high heat for 2 minutes, scraping up the brown bits from the bottom. Whisk the water and *Hot Sweet Mustard with Champagne* into the pan and simmer until reduced to about ⅓ cup. Add the butter, stirring until just incorporated. Season with salt and pepper. To serve, divide the arugula among four salad plates, top each plate with one-quarter of the scallops and spoon the sauce over the scallops. Sprinkle with fresh herbs. Serve with a loaf of crusty bread.

Serves 4 as a light lunch or a starter course

STONE GROUND MUSTARD WITH CABERNET

THIS WAS MADE WITH MY GRANDFATHER IN MIND. HE LOVED THE SEEDS IN HIS MUSTARD, AS WELL AS RED WINE AND GARLIC! USE THIS MUSTARD AS AN ACCOMPANIMENT TO STEAKS, PORK CHOPS, HAM, AND SAUSAGES. IT'S DELICIOUS IN VINAIGRETTES FOR SALADS, AND IN SAUCES FOR CHICKEN, SEAFOOD, OR EGGS.

ENLIGHTENED MUSTARD CREAM SAUCE

½ cup white wine

2 tablespoons shallots, finely minced

¾ cup chicken stock

1 tablespoon flour

2 tablespoons *Stone Ground Mustard with Cabernet*

¼ cup whipping cream

In a medium saucepan over high heat, combine the wine and shallots and bring to a boil, cooking until the liquid is almost evaporated.

Whisk together ¼ cup of the chicken stock and the flour; set aside. Add the remaining ½ cup chicken stock, bring to a simmer, and cook for 1 minute. Whisk in the *Stone Ground Mustard with Cabernet*, the cream, and the flour-and-stock mixture. Simmer for 2 minutes to blend the flavors and thicken sauce. Season with salt and pepper and serve.

Makes about 1¼ cups.

MEDITERRANEAN POTATO SALAD

Not your typical potato salad but what would you expect—it just screams picnic to me! This is also perfect to serve along with some grilled Cornish hens.

14-18 small red potatoes (about 2 pounds), quartered

¼ cup *Stone Ground Mustard with Cabernet*

¼ cup balsamic vinegar

4 small cloves garlic, minced

½ teaspoon salt (preferably kosher or sea salt)

Freshly ground pepper

½ cup extra-virgin olive oil

½ medium red onion, thinly sliced, soaked in water for 30 minutes, drained

½ cup diced kalamata olives

4 cups arugula (or baby spinach leaves)

Cook the potatoes in boiling, salted water for 6-8 minutes until tender. Whisk together the *Stone Ground Mustard with Cabernet*, vinegar, garlic, salt, pepper, and oil. Drain the potatoes and toss with two-thirds of the dressing. Stir in the onions, olives, and arugula and add more dressing if desired (I prefer lightly dressed salads). Serve warm or at room temperature.

Serves 4 to 6 as a side

PROSCIUTTO ROLLS

Here's an appetizer that not only tastes great but it looks really pretty—sushi-like rolls all standing upright—and it's a little different too!

- 3 tablespoons *Stone Ground Mustard with Cabernet*
- 4 ounces fresh soft goat cheese
- 8 thin slices prosciutto
- 16 pickled green beans, or pickled white asparagus, cut lengthwise into quarters
- 2 cups arugula

In a small bowl, mix the *Stone Ground Mustard with Cabernet* and the goat cheese. Spread each slice of prosciutto with the goat cheese mixture. Place four or five arugula leaves down the length of prosciutto, alternating the leaves top up and then top down, making sure the rounded edge of the leaf extends over the edges. Place a stack of 8 pieces of green beans at one end with the tops and bottoms extending over the edges. Make sure that some of the arugula and ends of green beans are sticking out on both ends.

Starting with the short side, roll it up and cut in half. Stand each roll up with the cut side down on a serving tray and the ruffled edge of the arugula and green beans jauntily extending upward.

Makes 16 pieces

EGGS NAPA WITH SPINACH & MUSTARD SAUCE

The first time I went to France, I was amazed that poached eggs in a variety of sauces were on the dinner menus. So my advice to you is, don't just save this for breakfast!

- 4 large eggs, poached
- 1 tablespoon olive oil
- 4 cups baby spinach
- Salt (preferably kosher or sea salt) and freshly ground pepper
- 4 slices whole-grain bread, toasted
- 1 recipe Enlightened Mustard Cream Sauce (see sidebar on opposite page)
- Fresh herbs or garlic flowers, for garnish

While the eggs are poaching, heat the oil in a large skillet over medium-high heat Add the spinach and a couple pinches of salt and pepper and sauté until the spinach just begins to wilt. Toast the bread. To serve, place a slice of toast on each of four warmed plates, top with a portion of spinach, a poached egg, and a couple spoonfuls of the sauce. Garnish with fresh herbs or garlic flowers.

Serves 4

Wine Suggestions

When accompanying steaks, pork, or sausages, this hedonistic mustard will team up expertly with big Napa Valley reds such as Cabernet Sauvignon, Merlot, Syrah and Zinfandel.

When served with poultry, seafood, or eggs the calling is for a sizeable, yet crisp white—a Sauvignon Blanc or un-oaked Chardonnay will be supreme.

Sunflowers

SPLASHES OF COLOR
THROUGHOUT THE GARDEN
REMINISCENT OF
GOLDEN CARAMEL,
DRIED CHERRIES,
AND CHOCOLATE

CHAPTER 11

Dessert Sauces

Vanilla Caramel Sauce with Chardonnay

Caramel Apple "Fondue"

Pear Tarts with Caramel Sauce

Banana-Pecan Crepes with Caramel Sauce

Caramelized Asian Chicken Wings

Chocolate Sauce with Cabernet

Gild-the-Lily Chocolate Fondue

Cabernet-Poached Pears with Chocolate Sauce

Warm Double-Chocolate Mini Cakes

Chocolate Bread Pudding with Dried Cherries

Chocolate Sauce with Kona

Chocolate-Dipped Pretzel Sticks

Individual Chocolate Soufflés with Warm Chocolate Sauce

Iced Mocha Latte

Sandwich Cookies with Chocolate & Pecans

JANE!®

This caramel sauce is sure to become one of your favorites, so much so that you might be tempted to eat it right out of the jar! The addition of Chardonnay sets this caramel sauce apart and gives it a nice buttery richness. Keep a jar or two on hand for quick and impressive desserts—spoon over ice cream and top with pecans and shaved chocolate or drizzle over angel food cake with blueberries, or brownies and ice cream for "turtle" sundaes.

CARAMEL APPLE "FONDUE"

2 large tart apples (Granny Smith or Pippin)

1 cup *Vanilla Caramel Sauce with Chardonnay*

¼ cup chopped salted peanuts

Cut the apples into wedges. Heat the *Vanilla Caramel Sauce with Chardonnay* in the microwave for 15-20 seconds for a pourable consistency. To assemble, place a small bowl or ramekin in the center of each of 4 dessert plates and fill each with about ¼ cup *Sauce*, top with 1 tablespoon of the nuts and circle the outside of the bowl with the apple wedges.

Each guest has a personal dessert fondue set-up — just dip an apple into the nuts and caramel and feel like a kid again!

Serves 4

PEAR TARTS WITH CARAMEL SAUCE

I used to be so afraid of any dish that called for puff pastry because I am not a baker. With frozen puff pastry, anyone can create fabulous desserts that your guests will think a pastry chef made, let's just keep this as our little secret!

1 sheet (about 8 ounces) frozen puff pastry, thawed

2 ripe pears (Anjou or Bartlett)

¼ cup plus 2 tablespoons sugar

1 teaspoon ground cinnamon

2 tablespoons melted butter

½ cup *Vanilla Caramel Sauce with Chardonnay*

Preheat the oven to 425°F. Line a large baking sheet with aluminum foil. Unfold the pastry sheet and cut in half. Place the first half between 2 sheets of plastic wrap and roll out to ⅛-inch thick, maintaining the rectangular shape. Remove the top sheet of plastic wrap and turn the pastry sheet onto one side of the baking sheet and remove the remaining sheet of plastic wrap. Repeat with the other half of the puff pastry sheet and place it next to the first half on the baking sheet. Trim any edges to even up the rectangles, if necessary. Brush the edges with water and turn over ½ inch all around. Dip the tines of a fork in flour and press them into the edges, sealing them all around.

Peel, halve, and core the pears, cut each half into ⅛-inch slices. In a medium bowl combine the pears slices, ¼ cup of the sugar, and the cinnamon. Toss to combine. Divide the pear slices between the two rectangles, slightly overlapping them to cover the pastry. Using a pastry brush, brush the edges of each tart with butter and place in the middle of the oven. Bake for 12-15 minutes until golden brown. Cut each tart into 6 pieces. Serve warm with a drizzle of *Vanilla Caramel Sauce with Chardonnay*. The sauce can be microwaved for 20-30 seconds for a pourable consistency. (The tarts can be made one day ahead and reheated in a 400°F oven for 5 minutes.)

Variation: For individual tarts, cut the pastry into 12 rectangles and follow the same directions as above.

Makes 2 regular tarts or 12 individual tarts

BANANA-PECAN CREPES WITH CARAMEL SAUCE

Your guests will be impressed with how beautiful and delicious your dessert is, and you will be thrilled with how little effort it takes. Add a little vanilla bean ice cream for an even more decadent dessert. You'll find the crepes in the produce section of your market.

4 tablespoons (½ stick) unsalted butter

4 medium-ripe bananas, peeled and cut in half lengthwise, then into ¼-inch slices

2 tablespoons brown sugar

1 teaspoon vanilla extract

½ cup chopped toasted pecans

8 prepared crepes

½ cup *Vanilla Caramel Sauce with Chardonnay*

Preheat the oven to 350°F. Melt the butter in a large skillet over medium heat. Add the bananas, brown sugar, vanilla, and ¼ cup of the pecans, stir to combine. Cook for 2 minutes, stirring occasionally, mashing the bananas slightly.

Lay 8 crepes out on your work surface. Place ⅛ of the banana mixture in the center of each crepe and spread it with the back of a spoon (it does not need to cover the whole crepe). Fold each crepe in half and then in half again, like a handkerchief. Place two crepes on each plate. Heat the *Vanilla Caramel Sauce with Chardonnay* in the microwave 15 to 20 seconds for a pourable consistency. Spoon the sauce over the crepes and top with the remaining pecans.

Serves 4

Wine Suggestions

The look, smell, and taste of caramel is heavenly with sweet, late-harvest wines. Caramel apple fondue is made for Late Harvest Riesling, and Pear tart is just the thing with a Sauternes or Botrytis Semillon. Pour a little sweet Muscat or Asti Spumante with the crepes. But with the chicken wings, serve a dry Gewürztraminer or Riesling.

CARAMELIZED ASIAN CHICKEN WINGS

When you think caramel sauce, you think dessert right? Well not necessarily. This savory dish combines caramel sauce with a little hot sauce to make a chicken dish that will blow your mind! I guarantee you this will be a favorite with your family and friends! Sriracha is a chile hot sauce available in the Asian sections of most large supermarkets and Asian markets-look for the rooster on the label.

½ cup *Vanilla Caramel Sauce with Chardonnay*

⅓ cup sriracha sauce

¼ cup soy sauce

2 pounds chicken wings or drumettes

Preheat the oven to 350°F. Combine the *Vanilla Caramel Sauce with Chardonnay*, the sriracha, and soy sauce in a large pan and heat over medium-high heat. Add the chicken wings and stir to coat well. Pour into a baking pan large enough to hold the chicken in a single layer. Cover with foil and bake for 30 minutes. Uncover, baste with the sauce, and cook for an additional 30 minutes, uncovered. Serve immediately.

Serves 4 generously as an appetizer

CHOCOLATE SAUCE WITH CABERNET

DARK CHOCOLATE PAIRED WITH CABERNET IS A DELICIOUS ENDING TO ANY MEAL. WE'VE COMBINED THE TWO INTO A SAUCE THAT YOU CAN USE TO FROST A CHOCOLATE CAKE WITH RASPBERRY FILLING, OR HEAT AND DRIZZLE OVER BROWNIES, DIP FRESH STRAWBERRIES, MAKE BANANA SPLITS OR CHOCOLATE SUNDAES. YOU KNOW THE DRILL.

GILD-THE-LILY CHOCOLATE FONDUE

Just about anything dipped in chocolate will taste divine! Fondue is such a fun dessert to serve.

Fill a platter with a gorgeous assortment of fresh fruits—whatever is in season—strawberries, orange and tangerine slices, ripe pears, bananas, pineapple, etc. Don't forget about dried fruits like figs and apricots. Include cubes of angel food or pound cake, or even shortbread cookies. Include caramels for dipping in the chocolate with a small crock of lavender sea salt to sprinkle on the chocolate-dipped caramels—now that is gild-the-lily fondue!

CABERNET-POACHED PEARS WITH CHOCOLATE SAUCE

Some things just go together, and pears, Cabernet, and chocolate is just one of those winning combinations! Definitely a Napa Valley favorite dessert! Leftover poaching syrup is delicious drizzled on ice cream.

> One 750 ml bottle red wine (Cabernet Sauvignon is suggested)
>
> 6 cups water
>
> 1½ cups sugar
>
> Peel of an orange
>
> Vanilla bean, halved lengthwise, (or use 1 tablespoon pure vanilla bean paste)
>
> Two 2-inch pieces of cinnamon stick
>
> 4 Bosc pears, slightly under ripe (peaches can be substituted in the summer)
>
> ½ cup *Chocolate Sauce with Cabernet*

Combine the wine, water, sugar, orange peel, vanilla bean, and cinnamon sticks in a large saucepan over medium-high heat and bring to a boil. Reduce heat to a simmer, and stir occasionally until the sugar has dissolved, about 10 minutes.

While the poaching liquid is heating, peel the pears, and with a melon baller remove the core by coming up from the bottom of the pear, scooping out the seeds and core. Add the pears to the poaching liquid making sure the pears are submerged. Bring the poaching liquid back to a boil, reduce the heat to a simmer, cover, and cook until the pears are tender, about 40 minutes. Remove the pears from the liquid, strain the poaching liquid, and pour it back into the pan. Bring to a boil, reduce heat to a simmer, and cook until the liquid is reduced by half and begins to get syrupy, about 30 minutes.

To assemble, warm the *Chocolate Sauce with Cabernet* in the microwave for 15-20 seconds until it is pourable. Cut each pear in half, and with cut side down cut each half into thin slices with the top end still intact so that you can fan out the pear. To serve, spoon a pool of the poaching syrup on each of four plates, top with a fanned pear half, drizzle with *Sauce*.

Serves 8

WARM DOUBLE-CHOCOLATE MINI CAKES

Oh my gosh, these are so unbelievably good, look fabulous and anyone can make them!

1 cup Chocolate Sauce with Cabernet

1 cup all-purpose flour

½ teaspoon baking soda

⅛ teaspoon salt (preferably kosher or sea salt)

6 ounces bittersweet or unsweetened chocolate chopped

8 tablespoons (1 stick) unsalted butter

¾ cup sugar

3 large eggs

1 teaspoon vanilla extract

½ cup milk

Confectioners' sugar

Fresh berries (strawberries, raspberries, blackberries, or a combination)

Preheat the oven to 350°F. Refrigerate the *Chocolate Sauce with Cabernet* for about 30 minutes. Butter and flour a muffin pan.

In a bowl, stir together the flour, baking soda, and salt. In a heavy saucepan, combine the chocolate and butter over low heat, stirring until melted. Set aside to cool. Beat together the sugar, eggs, and vanilla until foamy, about 3 minutes. Alternately add the flour mixture and milk, mixing after each addition until just blended. Stir in the melted chocolate. Fill the muffin cups two-thirds full with batter.

Using a teaspoon, scoop out a ball of chilled Sauce and place in the center of each muffin cup. Fill the muffin cups with the remaining batter. Bake for 12-15 minutes; the tops will be puffed but soft to the touch. Cool for 5 minutes, then invert onto a rack. Serve warm, sprinkled with confectioners' sugar and berries.

Makes 12

CHOCOLATE BREAD PUDDING WITH DRIED CHERRIES

This recipe is adapted from a dessert I had at Terra, one of my favorite restaurants in the Napa Valley. It's a perfect way to end a meal on a cold, winter night or any time really!

⅓ cup cognac

½ cup sun-dried cherries

1 cup *Chocolate Sauce with Cabernet*

3 large eggs

1 cup heavy cream

½ cup sour cream

½ cup sugar

⅛ teaspoon ground cinnamon

1 teaspoon vanilla extract

½ sourdough batard, crust removed and cut into ½-inch cubes, dried overnight

1 cup crème fraîche or sour cream

1 tablespoon confectioners' sugar, sifted

6 sprigs fresh mint

Combine the cognac and cherries, and soak for at least 2 hours or overnight. Melt the chocolate gently in a microwave. In a large bowl, whisk together the eggs, cream, sour cream, sugar, cinnamon, and vanilla. Whisk in the melted chocolate gently. Fold in the bread cubes, cherries, and cognac. Let sit in a warm place until the bread absorbs the custard, 1-2 hours. To test, break a bread cube in half; there should be no white showing. Spoon the mixture into an 8-cup soufflé dish or six 10-ounce dishes.

Preheat the oven to 350°F. Put the soufflé dish in a roasting pan and pour one-inch of boiling water into the pan. Carefully place in the oven and bake for 35-40 minutes, or until the pudding is puffed and set to touch. Let cool slightly.

Spoon portions of pudding onto individual plates. Whisk the confectioners' sugar into the crème fraîche, and top each portion with a large dollop. Garnish with mint.

Serves 6 to 8

The general guideline for pairing wines with chocolate is to serve a wine with at least as much sweetness as the chocolate itself. Consequently, a rich, ruby port (from California or Portugal) will set sail right on course.

However, we often relish sweet chocolate with the contrast of a dry, young red wine. In that case, a big, berry-scented Napa Valley Cabernet will be OH SO GOOD!

COMBINE DEEP DARK CHOCOLATE WITH THE RICH, DARK, EXOTIC FLAVOR OF KONA COFFEE AND YOU HAVE A MATCH MADE IN CHOCOLATE HEAVEN. SPOON SOME INTO YOUR MORNING LATTE FOR A MOCHA, SPREAD BETWEEN TWO VANILLA WAFERS AND ROLL IN CHOPPED NUTS FOR COOKIE SANDWICHES, OR DRIZZLE OVER A SCOOP OF ICE CREAM ATOP A BROWNIE.

CHOCOLATE-DIPPED PRETZEL STICKS

This is a fun treat to make with kids. Set up an assembly line with plates filled with all types of chopped nuts, colorful sprinkles, and chopped peppermints—get creative.

Look for the long pretzel rods or the shorter braided ones. Warm the *Chocolate Sauce with Kona* in the microwave for 15-20 seconds until it is of dippable consistency. Dip one end of each pretzel in the *Sauce* and then roll it in one of the toppings. Place the dipped pretzels in a short water glass with the dipped end up and let the chocolate cool. Serve the pretzels in colorful short glasses.

INDIVIDUAL CHOCOLATE SOUFFLÉS WITH WARM CHOCOLATE SAUCE

What a shame that soufflés were made out to be these very tricky desserts that could fall with the least little noise—not true! They couldn't be more delicious or easier to make and serve. Bet you can't eat just one!

> 1 tablespoon butter
> 1/3 cup sugar plus additional for sprinkling
> 1/2 cup *Chocolate Sauce with Kona*
> 3 large egg yolks, at room temperature
> 6 large egg whites
> Pinch of salt (preferably kosher or sea salt)

Preheat the oven to 375°F. Generously butter 6 individual ramekins, sprinkle with sugar, and tap out excess. Place of the *Chocolate Sauce with Kona* in a medium bowl and microwave for 20-30 seconds until it becomes pourable. Stir in the yolks, which will make the mixture stiffen. Beat the egg whites with a pinch of salt in a large bowl using an electric mixer at medium speed until they just form soft peaks. Add 1/3 cup sugar a little at a time until all of it is incorporated, and then beat at high speed until whites just form stiff peaks. Fold a third of the beaten egg whites into the chocolate mixture to lighten, then add the chocolate mixture to remaining whites, folding gently and mixing thoroughly.

Spoon the batter into ramekins, place on a baking sheet, and bake until puffed and crusted on top but still jiggly in center, 20 to 25 minutes. Five minutes before the soufflés are finished cooking, warm the remaining *Sauce* and pour into a small pitcher. Serve the soufflés hot from the oven and pass the *Sauce* for guests to pour into the center after they have broken through the top of the crust with a spoon.

Makes 6

ICED MOCHA LATTE

Need a pick-me-up? This will do it, I guarantee it!

> Brewed espresso, room temperature
> Chilled whole or non-fat milk
> 1 cup *Chocolate Sauce with Kona*

This recipe is based on individual taste. Select a beautiful drinking glass for serving. Spoon a tablespoon or two of *Chocolate Sauce with Kona* into the glass and a shot or two of espresso and stir to mix well. Fill the glass with ice and then pour the desired amount of milk into the glass and serve. We love to serve it with the Sandwich Cookies shown here.

SANDWICH COOKIES WITH CHOCOLATE & PECANS

Get the kids to make this dessert for you. They will have fun preparing these and they look really great piled up on a plate. At the holidays, use crushed candy canes instead of the pecans for a festive look.

> One 16-ounce package ginger cookies or vanilla wafers
> (look for small cookies 1 to 1½ inch in diameter)
> 1 cup of *Chocolate Sauce with Kona*, at room temperature
> ½ cup finely chopped pecans (or any nut of your choice)

Place half of the cookies on a work surface with bottom side facing up. Pour the nuts onto a plate. Using a table knife, spread a generous amount of *Chocolate Sauce with Kona* on each cookie, spreading to the edge. Top with the second cookie, bottom facing down and pressing together so that the *Sauce* oozes over the edges a bit. Roll the edge of the cookie sandwich in the nuts. For an adult treat, serve with our Iced Mocha Latte shown here.

Makes between 20 and 30 sandwich cookies

INDEX

✤